Royal Marines Musicians at War

This book is dedicated to those Royal Marines who freely gave their service and who then made the ultimate sacrifice.

Royal Marines Musicians at War

Brian Short

Pen & Sword
MILITARY

First published in Great Britain in 2025 by
Pen & Sword Military
An imprint of Pen & Sword Books Limited
Yorkshire – Philadelphia

ISBN 978 1 03611 282 0

A CIP catalogue record for this book is available from the British Library.

Typeset by Mac Style
Printed in the UK by CPI Group (UK) Ltd, Croydon, CR0 4YY.

FSC www.fsc.org MIX Paper | Supporting responsible forestry FSC® C013604

Pen & Sword Books Limited incorporates the imprints of After the Battle, Atlas, Archaeology, Aviation, Discovery, Family History, Fiction, History, Maritime, Military, Military Classics, Politics, Select, Transport, True Crime, Air World, Frontline Publishing, Leo Cooper, Remember When, Seaforth Publishing, The Praetorian Press, Wharncliffe Local History, Wharncliffe Transport, Wharncliffe True Crime and White Owl.

For a complete list of Pen & Sword titles please contact

PEN & SWORD BOOKS LIMITED
47 Church Street, Barnsley, South Yorkshire, S70 2AS, England
E-mail: enquiries@pen-and-sword.co.uk
Website: www.pen-and-sword.co.uk
or
PEN AND SWORD BOOKS
1950 Lawrence Road, Havertown, PA 19083, USA
E-mail: uspen-and-sword@casematepublishers.com
Website: www.penandswordbooks.com

Contents

Foreword

Musicians have been going to war since the days of antiquity. Their deeds are even covered in the Old Testament. It was the sound of trumpets that brought down the walls of Jericho. Less dramatic is one of my favourite Kipling short stories, 'The Drums of the Fore and Aft'. The nautical terms 'fore' and 'aft' in the title have no maritime connotations, being instead the nickname bestowed on an imaginary British Army regiment that retreated ignominiously during a battle on the Northwest Frontier of late Victorian India. The heroes of the story are two drummer boys, Lew and Jakin, both aged about 14. These two, one with a side drum, the other with a fife, march out alone towards the tribesmen massed on a plain to their front, playing 'The British Grenadiers'. Their regiment, shamed by the courage of the two boys, leave the gully where they have been cowering after a good pasting by the tribesmen and take their bayonets to the queen's enemies. The boys are killed during the ensuing melee. The story has a typical Kiplingesque ending:

> Some say, and among these are the Gurkhas who watched on the hillside, that that battle was won by Jakin and Lew, whose little bodies were borne up just in time to fill two gaps at the head of the big ditch-grave for the dead under the heights of Jagai.

The ancestors of today's Royal Marines drummers have been going to war since 28 October 1664, when, as Brian Short relates, King Charles II at a meeting of the Privy Council directed that 1,200 land soldiers be raised and distributed into His Majesty's Fleets; formed into six companies, each company to have one drummer. The regiment was raised as the Duke of York and Albany's Maritime Regiment of Foot. Because James, Duke of York was Lord High Admiral, it came also to be known as the Admiral's Regiment. The drummers would have beaten the men of the regiment to quarters (action stations) on their drums at its first engagement in the sea battle against the Dutch fleet off Lowestoft in 1665. The regiment was first mentioned as Marines after the battle against the Dutch in Sole Bay. Lord Arlington's secretary wrote: 'Those Marines of whom I so often have wrote you, behaved themselves stoutly.'

A well-known painting of the 2nd Marine Battalion at the Battle of Bunker Hill in 1775 shows the drummer beating out the step, one of the key roles performed by the drummer in land engagements. By the middle of the eighteenth century, bugle calls had replaced drum calls in many regiments fighting on land because they could be heard more clearly than drum rolls against the noise of battle. However, drum calls continued to be used at sea until the mid- to late nineteenth century.

Brian Short has mentioned my connection with the Royal Marines Band Service, starting with my time as a house officer at the Royal Marines School of Music at the RM Depot at Deal in the late 1950s/early 1960s. Under this system, lieutenants in their mid- to late twenties, usually with combat experience, were appointed to take charge of houses – exactly like housemasters at fee-paying private schools. This was rewarding and fun, as it included taking one's house camping, and hard-fought inter-house competitions. Several senior officers of the corps, including some general officers, had been house officers in their younger days. It was by no means a 'dud' posting; the opposite, in fact. One came to appreciate the talent in the Band Service and I acquired some understanding of what motivated these talented musicians.

Brian Short's *Musicians Who Went to War* is a wonderful account of the military deployments in the twentieth and twenty-first centuries undertaken by the best military band in the world, written by a Royal Marine musician who participated in some of them. The musical performance of Royal Marines bands, especially the vocal, and string and woodwind sections, has been greatly enriched since the late twentieth century by including females in the Band Service. These smart and immaculate female musicians are an inspiration.

A significant feature of the Royal Marines Band Service is their role in conflict at all levels of intensity where they back up the medical services and provide armed security at key locations in the combat zone. To this end, musicians are trained in the handling of a variety of infantry weapons and undergo instruction and exercises in field conditions under the tutelage of Royal Marines weapons instructors.

From time to time, the future existence of Royal Marines bands is questioned by politicians. They should read this book; perhaps they will come to appreciate what a splendid contribution the Royal Marines Band Service has made to our country, by land and sea, and will continue to do so.

Major General Julian Thompson, CB, OBE, Royal Marines (Retired)
Commander 3rd Commando Brigade RM
Falklands War, 1982

Introduction

I do accept that the rather strident title of this book might suggest that The Bands of His Majesty's Royal Marines are in an almost permanent state of combat readiness, and in almost constant danger as they tour the world, ready at a moment's notice to take on our foreign adversaries. If that is what the title has led you to believe then apologies for the slight misdirection, but as you read on, I think you will find that their music, their history, and the military service that these superb musicians have collectively given over the years will impress you, as will their achievements and their losses.

Before I continue, I really must take this opportunity to thank Major General Julian Thompson, CB, OBE, Royal Marines, for kindly agreeing to write the foreword for this book. His heartfelt and insightful words I think show the high regard and support he has for the Royal Marines Band Service (RMBS). Having had contact with the Band Service early in his career, and having seen their work through The Falklands and beyond, he was once again the obvious choice to ask to contribute a foreword, and once again, he has delivered in his inimitable and thoughtful style.

I also need to thank Mr John Ambler, the very knowledgeable and unofficial historian of the RMBS, who has kindly given permission for me to use his *Royal Marines Band Service* book as reference material, for which I am most grateful.

The Royal Marines are no doubt famous for many things, but perhaps the two elements that would be uppermost in the public's mind are the Royal Marines Commandos and the Royal Marines Band Service. Both have a worldwide reputation – the green beret Commandos as some of the finest (if not *the* finest) troops in the world, and the band as some of the best (if not *the* best) military musicians on planet Earth. Now, these statements might be regarded as bold and subjective, but they do hold up to objective scrutiny, and there are many people, both friend and foe, who would either happily agree with them or, perhaps having been on the receiving end of the Royal Marines' attention, grudgingly acknowledge them. Both these professional branches of the Royal Marines Corps live symbiotically, side by side, each acknowledging the professional skill set of the other, with the Commando branch recognising the publicity and profile-raising value of their musicians, and the Band Service recognising the professional way the Commandos can deliver violence to our adversaries in times of need – something that is also recognised by our enemies, NATO colleagues and even sometimes, our politicians. What both branches of the Royal Marines have in common is that they strive for excellence in whatever they do, and through good leadership, training and that famous cap badge ethos, they seldom miss the mark; being *just* good enough is not good enough for a Royal Marines instructor or training team member.

The famous Globe & Laurel cap badge.

Having established the mutual respect each branch has for the other and the firm demarcation of their respective roles, this book will also outline the many non-musical and military operational roles the RMBS has undertaken in its lifetime and some of the achievements and losses it has incurred as a result. The reverse idea of giving Commando ranks instruments has never really been explored, which comes as something of great relief to members on both sides of the divide. There are one or two notable exceptions: first, there is a well-known former Commando jazz saxophonist in the West Country, and an equally well-known Commando accordion player musically terrorising the Taunton area. This former Royal Marines SBS operator will, without warning, launch into various obscure sea shanties at mess dinners, until fellow diners eventually disarm him and the offending accordion is wrestled back into its case. This gentleman also did some time as the regimental sergeant major (RSM) at the Royal Marines School of Music in Deal, which might account for his musical leanings. I ought to point out that, in this instance, SBS does not refer to the 'Special Band Service' but to a well-known Special Forces branch of the Royal Marines – the Special Boat Service.

As with all hard and fast rules, my book research did reveal there is one exception to the above grand statement that needs acknowledgement, that being 42 Commando Royal Marines Pipe Band. Just why 42 Commando Royal Marines needed a bagpipe band, armed with the 'Jockanese Porridge Gun', will become clearer when you see that the Royal Marines have had a long association with Scotland; they have always trained there and the Commando memorial proudly sits at Spean Bridge in the Highlands for all to see. Add to this a long line of proud Scots who have joined the corps and I think you can understand how it was perhaps inevitable that the bagpipes would infiltrate their way into the Royal Marines at some point.

The Pipe Band was first started informally to provide music when the Commando unit was deployed abroad and for which no official RM band of the time could provide music. Initiated by a Scots Royal Marines officer, volunteers were sought, drums were bashed, and pipes were blown and squeezed by Commando Marines until at some point, enough progress was made for them to be released onto a parade ground. Eventually, having proven their worth and gained traction with senior officers, the Band Service was able to give some support by supplying members of the Buglers Branch on detached duty to lead and instruct on drums and bagpipes. Several names appear time and again in recognition of this support, Sergeant Bugler Reginald Flook being instrumental in keeping the Pipe Band going by volunteering for a lengthy deployment with 42 Commando to continue his work with them as 'Pipe Major', a rank and title that does not really exist in the Royal Marines. Other notable personnel are Buglers Alan Piner and George Coad, both legendary figures in the Band Service of their day – Piner for his creative drum solo compositions, and Coad for telling more tales than Beatrix Potter. The late George Coad appears again in this book in the firefighting section but was such a huge character that he really deserved a chapter of his own. So, with the reluctant acceptance that at certain points in time Royal Marines Commandos have committed acts of music, generally, highly technical musical skill has been left to the Royal Marines Band Service.

The aim of this book is, through research and, where possible, personal testimony, to examine some of the many non-musical deployments that the RMBS has taken part in, and by 'taken part', I mean arrived with their boots on to get stuck into whatever military tasks they were detailed to undertake rather than having arrived as musicians to play or entertain. For the most part, it might at first seem that the 'Bandies' will have undertaken medical duties, but there are plenty of instances of musicians being issued weapons for more military duties, such as guarding prisoners, flying in helicopters into hot landing zones, and driving combat vehicles in places detrimental to one's health. They have also operated military equipment far more complicated than a B-flat valve trombone or a hand-tuned timpani.

As a branch of the Royal Marines, when required the RMBS are expected to contribute more than music to an operation, and hopefully through this book you will gain some insight into what has sometimes been asked of them and how they have delivered. There are also some surprises amongst their many and varied tasks, from assisting the local police to being co-opted as rescuers on both land and sea – perhaps a timely reminder of the Royal Marines motto, '*Per Mare, Per Terram*' (By Sea, By Land).

Just in case you might be one of the few unfortunate people who are not familiar with the modern-day Royal Marines Band Service, let me broadly outline them in a short paragraph. In their ceremonial blue uniforms and striking white helmets, at humour as disrespect for those I am writing about; we all come from similar backgrounds and share a common and sometimes dark sense of humour.

The musicians I write about are worthy of respect and recognition for taking on the challenges that military operations have thrown at them over the years, and whilst smiling in the face of adversity, have come out the other side. Humour, it seems, even dark humour, is important in the military world to help overcome some of the terrible and dangerous things we ask of our people, perhaps even more so post traumatic event, which luckily in these more enlightened times is recognised. Musicians have honed their own slightly skewed sublayer of humour that works well in the music world, but also can be enjoyed in the wider world if you care to partake. To that end, each of the respondents who gave me details of their operations also included some humorous occurrence that took place – in Royal Marines slang, 'a dit'. Where the 'dit' has been deemed funny or suitable for publication, without fear of prosecution, it is included in the relevant chapter.

I am extremely grateful to each of those who responded and gave me their time, thoughts, feelings and photographs. There are far too many names to list in an introduction page, so apologies for putting you all together in one special respondents' page at the end of the book. Think of it as a reunion of sorts, but on paper, in the back of a book, which hopefully, you have bought and you are currently reading.

In concluding this introduction I must say that this is not a history book and I am definitely not a historian. It is not meant to be read as historically accurate reference material, but more of a book that chronicles the memories of those musicians who were deployed outside of their musical role and the notable events that were important enough for them to be remembered. My purpose has been to research and collate these memories, and then gather them together in one place before they are lost forever. Far too many members of the Royal Marines Band Service have already died without anyone knowing of the small or sometimes large contributions that they made in times of need. Hopefully, this book redresses that imbalance to some degree.

Finally, given my limited intellect, numerical dyslexia and poor administrative skills, there will be some errors, mistakes and, worse still, some omissions within this book, for which I accept full responsibility. Writing a book is not quite as easy as both you and I might think.

Chapter One

Drummers, Buglers and Musicians

In writing this book and including many references to drummers, buglers and musicians, it occurs to me that an explanation is in order to correctly identify one from the other, as well as to reveal something of their heritage and, in fact, the very reason for their existence. It is a story that starts a long time ago, right back to the very beginnings of the Royal Marines, before they became 'Royal' and even before they became 'marines'. Read on…

On 28 October 1664, an order was issued by an Order in Council in Whitehall for 1,200 soldiers to be recruited to serve aboard the fleet. We are, after all, an island nation and the protection of the home shores and assets abroad needed consideration. In attendance at this meeting was King Charles II, who approved

Modern RM drummers wearing uniform of the 1664 period. (*Paul Meacham*)

the formation of the Duke of York and Albany's Maritime Regiment of Foot. As well as officers, sergeants and fighting soldiers, the signed order took care to include that one other particular specialised rank was needed for this regiment, namely, a drummer for each company of men. This traces the provenance of the drummer, bugler and musician back to day one of the Royal Marines Corps that we know today. It is to this formation order and humble beginnings that the modern-day Royal Marines Band Service can trace its heritage back to the fighting marines of that first regiment in 1664.

The reason for the inclusion of a drummer was not so those early marines could dance with each other – no; that would come much later! It was, of course, important in that era of warfare to have an audible way of transferring orders in the melee of battle, so the young drummers of yore were important to the fight. That also meant they had to be much closer to the action than a modern reader might imagine a drummer needed to be. When a senior officer in a field battle gave an order, it was cascaded down the rank structure, and in places shouted man to man. But potentially, an order beaten out by a drummer could be recognisable above the din of battle, and therefore advances or retreats made in quick or at least quicker time, dependent, of course, on the skill and volume of the particular drummer. There were also more routine tasks for the drummers, such as summoning troops back into barracks or camp at the end of the day's fighting or, in some cases, drinking.

So, with music in general and drummers in particular being deemed essential to the military machine, the early pre-Band Service continued to grow in numbers, instruments and importance in line with the Duke of York and Albany's Regiment. No doubt, many drummers played a part as the Marines fought their early battles all around the world – and it is the extent of their involvement in conflicts far and wide that eventually led to the globe being incorporated into the design for their renowned cap badge. If any reader knows of or has worn what they believe to be a more distinguished cap badge, then I would be delighted to hear of it – which of course is just another inter-service pigtail-pulling iteration on my part.

To continue with this potted history, in 1802, after 138 years of far-reaching, meritorious service, His Majesty King George III honoured them with the official title of Royal Marines, thereby giving them the recognition for their many hard-earned battle honours. The term 'Royal' eventually came into common parlance as one of the many nicknames given to the Marines by their Royal Navy counterparts. Other nicknames abounded from our matelot kinsmen – some not necessarily suitable for publication or use at family gatherings – but in general, on a navy ship, 'Royal' or 'Booties' is the accepted terminology.

This short but important account of the birth of the Royal Marines is used to illustrate that once you have the first 'marines', you also have the first marine

RM drummers wearing period uniform, as they would have in Nelson's era. (*Paul Meacham*)

musicians, even if they were not 'Royal' at that time and were confined to marching drums. Perhaps you are one of those people that find difficulty in accepting drummers as musicians. As a drummer myself, I can categorically state that yes, we are, and yes, you most definitely should.

Having described the evolution of those early marine drummers now is a good time to note the differences between them and the musicians of the current RMBS. As I have already explained, along with the formation of those first 'marines' came the need for the first drummers, who for many years were the sole musical

RM buglers as they are now – happy to lead the band or perform on stage. Note the thin stripe on their uniform trousers, depicting their heritage. (*Paul Meacham*)

participants in military warfare. At some point, someone had the idea that perhaps a more strident horn or bugle tone might provide a more piercing and attention-grabbing way of sounding orders. This had an additional benefit of cutting down on some of the incessant 'tap-tapping' that everyone who knows a drummer must put up with. Eventually, the drum and the bugle were combined into one role within the Royal Marines, evolving into the buglers we see today marching at the front of the modern RM bands. The Buglers Branch of the Band Service take their early heritage seriously and this is reflected in their uniform, on the trousers of which they wear a thin red stripe as opposed to the thick red stripe of the musicians marching behind them.

For added clarity, and because I was one of the chosen few, there is another kind of drummer in the RMBS – the percussionists. These unusual and talented drummers are few in number but are expected to master the full range of percussion instruments, from the xylophone to the drum kit, and all manner of 'bangy' instruments in between. They will on occasion strap on a marching snare drum and can sometimes be seen in the second rank of drums, following the front rank of buglers on parade. Percussionists are also classed as 'musicians' and therefore wear the thick red stripe on their trousers. So, if you were in any doubt, it is official: drummers are musicians!

In the Royal Marines, the title bugler or musician can also be their rank; in layman's terms, they are equivalent to a private in the army. In this book, the catch-all term 'musicians' refers to all ranks of the Royal Marines Band Service, regardless of them being categorised as a musician or a bugler. Notwithstanding the thickness of the red stripe on their uniform, I will at times refer to them all in general terms as musicians. I know there will be traditional members of the Buglers Branch who will be indignant at this outrageous proposal, and in a skewed sense of identity (and with the cock crowing three times) will be denying this bestowed honorary title in favour of 'bugler'. I accept and look forward to pointed fingers and general abuse at future reunions – from buglers and musicians one and all!

In the beginning, as the need grew for more drummers, so did the requirement for more musicians to accompany them. Bugles, fifes and eventually other brass and woodwind instruments were introduced, until the modern military bands that we are now familiar with became the norm. This was not of course restricted to just the early Royal Marines but was emulated and repeated across the whole of the British military of the time, with the army also having its long heritage of musical progression. There are some important differences between the army (Royal Corps of Army Music) and the Royal Marines music services, and the way they train and perform, both in music and on operations. However, in modern times, there is certainly much better cooperation and professional mutual respect for the quality of music produced on both sides, and in that, I also include the highly regarded Royal Air Force Music Services. If one could be subjectively considered better than the others, then the reader will have to refer to their own cap badge history, and their musical ear, to decide. (On reading this back, not only did I fall off the impartiality fence, I think I may have taken some of you down with me.)

This chapter serves to give a brief history and background to the formation of Royal Marines music. A full and detailed account of how the early drummers, buglers and eventually musicians evolved into the modern Royal Marines Band Service has been well documented by historian and author John Ambler. John is a member of the Royal Marines Historical Society and has chronicled the history of the Band Service in several volumes of his book *The Royal Marines Band Service* as well as in many well-researched articles. John has graciously given me permission to quote from his book, saying, 'There's no point in reinventing the wheel!' I hope in the writing I have not just reinvented the wheel, but added a few more spokes and a playing card attached to the rim for added effect.

Chapter Two

A Musician with a Gun

Before getting into the meat of the book about musicians' military deployments, I think it is worth discussing just how, why and when a military musician might be given a gun. The how, why or when they might be armed and operationally deployed depends on a host of factors, not least of which is what branch of the armed forces they belong to. In the Royal Marines Band Service, the musicians are Royal Marines first, but their professional trade is one of music, so although the military skills they are taught are thorough and deeply ingrained, they are also limited.

Before they even get to play a musical instrument at the Royal Marines School of Music (RMSM) in Portsmouth, they must first report for initial basic training at the Commando Training Centre (CTCRM) at Lympstone in Devon. Their training covers all the basics of any new recruit into the armed forces, including marching, fitness, weapon handling and basic infantry skills, as well as the basics and some of the knowledge required to live out in the field. It is not a mini Commando course but is nevertheless taught by Royal Marines Commando instructors. It is both exacting and deliberately arduous so as to test the trainees and also give them some idea of the standards expected of anyone aspiring to wear the Globe & Laurel cap badge.

Given that these young trainee musicians are generally fresh out of school or, if a little older, will still have only limited experience in the civilian world, the shock of military capture is a wake-up call and sharp introduction to life in the Royal Marines. It is something they must get through before they can get back to playing music, and so the pressure is on but the incentives are high. There are not too many failures at this stage, mostly because at the pre-joining music auditions there are also physical tests to pass, which expose them to the full-on physical training instructors (PTIs) and show up any fitness weakness or issues they must address if accepted for service. This gives the motivated individual time to up their fitness level before getting to CTCRM, thereby avoiding a rude awakening and replacing it with just an awakening. From my own experience of promotion courses and military training at CTCRM, due to the nature of the beast no one is deemed fit enough by any of the training teams on day one, and you need to do more than merely pass a test to get credit or even an acknowledgement.

Once there, for most of the trainees it will be the first time they will have handled a weapon and certainly the first time they will have handled one the Royal Marines way. Having the pressure of a weapons instructor breathing down their necks as they first carry out the dry drills and then when they eventually fire a weapon takes more than a little getting used to. Hands normally accustomed to delicately stroking a violin bow or pushing down a trumpet valve now find themselves pushing rounds into a weapon magazine on a cold day, with fingers sometimes trapped in the working parts if wrongly handled. Some take to this quite readily, but then there always seems to be one who presents the instructor with certain issues that need to be addressed. I initially struggled with 'certain issues' but by the end of my training at Deal, I was so proficient with a rifle that I beat all comers in the annual unit shoot. Now and forevermore, my name is etched on the shooting trophy called The Haughton Cup. (This boastful fact of course bears no relation to this book, but with no one in my family being the least bit interested, I just wanted to tell someone.)

Assuming that the junior musician passes all the military tests, they are then sent back to the Royal Marines School of Music in Portsmouth to continue their musical training. The school of music is housed in the former Royal Navy detention quarters and retains some of the features of a military jail. One of the most obvious is that the cells are now individual practice rooms, where the musician can blow and bang away without disturbing nearby 'cellmates'. In November 2023, Anne, Princess Royal officially opened The Alford Schools of Military Music in Portsmouth, which trains musicians for both the Royal Marines and the British Army. During the previous year, the army had lost their prestigious Kneller Hall music training facility in Richmond upon Thames due to financial cutbacks, hence the move to Portsmouth. Being in close proximity to the RMSM, it was deemed feasible to share some music training facilities under the umbrella of the newly named Alford School of Music but to continue to train separately and maintain their own identities, standards and ethos. Incidentally, the new facility is named after Kenneth J. Alford, a British composer of marches who served as a bandmaster in both the British Army and the Royal Marines, and who is most famously remembered for his 'Colonel Bogey March'.

Having achieved the high musical standards required at the RMSM, once the trainee musicians are deemed ready, and with their final exams behind them, they are sent out into the real world to join one of the Royal Marines bands around the country. This may sound like the end of their musical training but actually, it is just the beginning as they continue to broaden their musical knowledge. It is also the start of their Royal Marines career, wider experiences and, in due course, annual military training.

The on-the-job experience of playing for live audiences and exposure to new music is a learning curve, as is the immersion into the military way of life. What still may come as something of a shock to the young musicians is that there are a couple of weeks each year when they must stow their musical instrument and pick up a weapon to refresh or relearn those military skills taught during initial training. Apart from the generic military skills everyone must maintain, each Royal Marines band has a wartime role for which they must put time aside each year to practise. Regardless of whether it is a medical role, key point guarding or a more specific tasking, there will also be time for physical and weapons refresher training on the range. Generally speaking, these training weeks are not something to be enjoyed but to be got through with good grace and humour, which can be more palatable if you are lucky enough to get a Commando training team that knows the Bandies' skills. There are times when humour helps, such as during one range firing day when an RM Commando sergeant asked the band to judge the distance to a target. A band corporal volunteered, stepped forth and taking an imaginary golf swing, replied, 'That's about a five iron,' which brought a smile to even the sergeant's craggy face – but also a set of press-ups to the corporal's golf-swinging arms.

Another notable feature of Band Service range days is the zeroing of weapons to suit the individual's stance, grip and sight picture. It involves firing the rifle with the weapons instructor carefully adjusting the rifle sights to correct the aim of the shooter. Unfortunately, on one occasion (and many others), by the end of the shoot the instructor was less than pleased to find that the band had, in order to reduce weapon cleaning time, been passing the same two weapons around the forty members, therefore making the zeroing redundant.

Now that you know how they have weapons, the question of why musicians of any ilk should be considered for deployment into a theatre of operations comes down to a few simple equations. First, manpower, which ultimately can be traced back to money and budgets. In times of peace, politicians rarely increase defence budgets, so there is a decreasing amount of money, and therefore people, to do whatever tasking is required. In modern times, there have been many defence reviews and moratoriums where the very existence of military music has come into question, so the way to help justify the bands' continuation to the politician or bean-counting accountant is for them to have a dual role. This can take many forms, but in general, it is in the secondary line as medical assistant, orderlies, stretcher-bearers or in the supply chain as drivers. This list is not exhaustive and is usually expanded upon in theatre as the command hierarchy recognise the added skill set brought by musicians, along with their intelligence and good humour, which can be applied in most situations to everyone's benefit.

As you will read throughout this book, RMBS ranks will have also found themselves carrying weapons and in situations well outside their comfort zones – situations that will not have been mentioned to them by any careers sergeant when they first entered a military careers office. There have been many occasions when they have found themselves armed in operational theatres, and whilst not expected to get involved with section attacks and balcony abseiling anti-terrorist exploits, they have had to act quickly, positively, and sometimes aggressively to fulfil their duties. Acting as armed guards on a gate, guarding a key point or keeping control over prisoners of war – as some of us did during the Falklands War – has required the musician to adjust their mindset and remember their training, as well as their cap badge and the ethos behind it. Could and would a musician pull a trigger to end a life? It is a question for the individual but once you have had to consider it, then I believe yes, most of us would.

Not surprisingly in a book of this nature, I find myself writing the word 'musician' a great deal and deliberately not the word 'bandsman', so I feel the need to explain the difference in terminology. I am not usually a snob or sniffy about titles, but somehow the training and role of the modern RMBS deserves the highest informal acknowledgement it can get, and if that has to start with names, then musicians they are. A more modern 'woke' author might also point out that 'bandsman' is a little antiquated and does not recognise the proper naming and contribution of females to the modern RMBS and to military music. Regarding genders, I have grown up with two, but it appears many others are now readily available. I am not that 'woke' author but am happy to adjust my mindset when required. So, depending on *when* you are reading this, the term 'musicians' also encompasses all available serving genders. Any questions?

This chapter has outlined why musicians sometimes have to be deployed into theatres of conflict and are sometimes issued weapons. It is not their natural environment but one in which they seem to readily adapt and impress those with whom they have contact. Over the years, some have referred to a rifle as a gun and called ammunition rounds bullets, but this is usually for the benefit of a hardened Commando platoon weapons instructor (PWI) who needed educating into the mindset and humour of a 'bandy'.

As a parting shot (pun intended) regarding guns in particular, I would say that the Band Service has produced some excellent shooters, some of whom have represented the corps at prestigious competitions such as Bisley. Some others, however, would have struggled to hit a cow's arse with a banjo, even if they were both in the back of a Mini together. So, when you are deploying Royal Marines musicians to a theatre of operations and they are expected to be carrying weapons, the attendant Commando ranks should anticipate seeing the full range of weapon handling abilities within the band, starting with cautious, low expectations, but also happy to be pleasantly surprised by some deft stoppage drills and post-shooting good cleaning technique … assuming, of course, they have not shared their weapons as before!

Band Colour Sergeant Steve 'Rasher' Bacon, pictured during Operation Herrick in Afghanistan.

Chapter Three

World Wars: Musicians at Sea

With the light-heartedness of the opening chapters behind us, it is time to turn to the more serious subject matter of the book – Royal Marines musicians at war. It might seem disingenuous to try to describe in one chapter the many years of the bands' active service duty in both of the world wars; and their service, sacrifice and accompanying losses deserve remembering and recording with better writing then I am capable of. However, I will take a broad-brush approach so that the uninitiated will have something of an understanding of the Band Service history of those times, and if you feel the need, you can delve deeper into the subject by referencing John Ambler's excellent books.

An innocuous Admiralty Order issued in 1910 required musicians who were being drafted to ships to attend a fire control course at the Royal Navy Gunnery School in Portsmouth. Since this was peacetime and prior to an exciting ship draft, I can imagine a young musician, at best, finding the course interesting, or, at worst, just something to be got through before joining their ship and sailing for ports exotic, alcohol various and female relationships of the brief kind.

The course syllabus came from the RN Gunnery training manual and would be familiar to many former sailors of that era, along with a particular style of instruction and correction from the imposing RN Gunnery officers of the day! Gunnery officers were (and probably still are) less known for their humour and more for their disciplined gun drills and work ethic, so what they made of intelligent young musicians under their instruction is not recorded.

The course consisted of learning to operate a selection of rangefinding and deflection equipment, to enable battleship guns to track and accurately fire at the enemy. It required teamwork to operate what was, in effect, a rudimentary manually operated computer, which once it had all the information dialled in would give the Gunnery officers the information they needed to aim and range the guns. The band and musicians got this job because even back then, it was recognised that musical intellect (a phrase coined and oft repeated by me in this book), or the 1910 equivalent, gave the team something of a head start as they orchestrated the information and machinery to produce a good firing solution. This would have been all well and good in peacetime, albeit in hot and uncomfortable conditions, but in wartime, the situation and stakes were obviously much higher, as you and your shipmates' lives could depend on it.

In 1914, the First World War began and the Royal Navy, its sailors and musicians would be sorely tested. The navy still had hundreds of ships in its fleet at this time, with a small ship's band on many of the medium to larger vessels, so a great many musicians would find themselves at sea for extended periods. As well as their musical duties, they were trained for their action stations gunnery role. For various technical and design reasons, their duty station was usually well below decks, presumably to protect it from being hit and damaged by the enemy. However, this also meant that there were many bulkheads and sealed hatches between their action station and the open deck, so escaping would have been difficult at the best of times. During the worst of times in battle, damage to decks from exploding shells and torpedoes could warp bulkheads, causing hatches to be wedged closed, blocking any escape and sealing the fate of those below.

Sadly, a great many RMBS ranks were lost in the First World War in this way; in total, 204 musicians and buglers would never return from their sea service, their names being recorded in the roll of honour. When writing and reading about wars, statistics and remembering the dead, it can be all too easy to forget that these were all real people, and their duty and sacrifice lost in the sea of all the other millions who died. We often say at remembrance services, 'We shall remember them', and perhaps sometimes we do, especially if there is a connection or a photograph. So, to put at least one face to the number included here is the name and picture of Boy Bugler Charles Ernest Timmins who, at the tender age of 14, was the youngest Royal Marine to be killed in the First World War. He was killed doing his duty as he sounded the 'Alert' bugle call aboard HMS *Cardiff* while she was under fire. Fortunately, perhaps, if there is ever such a thing in war, he was killed instantly when a shell hit the ship and a piece of shrapnel pierced his heart. I hope by remembering this one short life, active service and ultimately his death while carrying out his duty, this serves to remind us of the many other buglers and musicians who had their lives cut short on active

Bugler Timmins is commemorated in this depiction of him doing his final duty.

Timmins's baby-faced joining-up picture.

service at sea. The loss of a young son in any circumstances is tragic, but Bugler Timmins's family would endure another devastating loss when a short time later, his father was also killed at sea serving aboard HMS *Hogue*.

In memory of Bugler Charles Ernest Timmins, and all of those poor souls lost in the First World War, surviving Band Service members made voluntary donations to procure a set of silver memorial drums, including one bass drum and five side drums. The bass drum has the names of the many men lost emblazoned upon it, whilst the five side drums record the names of the ships on which they were lost.

One can only imagine the relief felt by those serving on ships when the Armistice was signed and the long war was at last over. It meant a return to the relatively peaceful days of life at sea, playing music when required and visiting exotic ports for exotic things! Pay and conditions may not have been ideal, but at least no one was trying to kill them, and they still had their daily issue of Pusser's Rum to take the edge off their shipmate's snoring in the next bunk or hammock. (A quick side note to mourn 'Black Tot Day' when, on 31 July 1970, the last daily rum ration was issued in the Royal Navy.)

The period following the end of the First World War might have seemed idyllic for a young musician at sea, but within a few short years, dark clouds of war were once again gathering over Europe and, as the Second World War gathered pace, would spread around the world. Once again, military musicians would be put in harm's way.

When the Second World War began, the Royal Navy was still one of the most powerful navies in the world, with over 200,000 officers, sailors and Royal Marines serving in the fleet. The navy had 15 battleships, with 5 more being built, 7 aircraft carriers, 66 cruisers, 184 destroyers, 60 submarines and 45 smaller escort and patrol vessels. These numbers quickly increased as urgent war building got underway and Lend Lease naval options were taken up from the USA. This made for a formidable fleet, with most of the larger ships and aircraft carriers having a ship's band amongst their complement.

Like their forebears in the Great War, the Second World War musicians undertook plotting duties in what was known as the Transmitting Station (TS), which for all the same reasons was buried deep within the bowels of those huge battleships. One

The memorial drums commemorating all those musicians who lost their lives in the First World War serving aboard ships.

unnamed bugler recorded his experience of being in the transmitting station when his ship, HMS *Cleopatra*, was torpedoed. The weapon hit close to his station and the noise, heat and confusion were greatly added to when the ship listed 45 degrees. Just imagine the surreal sights, sounds and horror of being in that predicament, locked below many decks of battened-down hatches. Reading the account, the relief is palpable as he recalls his petty officer shouting, 'Right lads, up top as fast as you can go,' thereby releasing them from their duty, and physically releasing them from their action station. Later, he writes about volunteering to help recover the dead and wounded from the damaged engine room compartments, again showing great courage and depth of character as he searches for his lost shipmates, not knowing that some of them were already dead. With his ship putting into Valetta harbour in Malta for repairs, he writes that as the duty bugler he played the 'Last Post' at his band and shipmate's burials, which must have been a very solemn occasion. I have attended burials at sea of fallen Royal Marines and marvelled at how our buglers maintain their composure to play in such overwhelmingly difficult and emotional circumstances. In this one attack on HMS *Cleopatra*, twenty-three sailors and one musician were killed – yet more names to be added to memorials, family histories and thoughts on remembrance days. This story resonates with me as I recall that during the Falklands War, Sergeant Bugler John Tansey volunteered to attend to the bodies of four deceased Royal Marines and prepare them for burial at sea. It was an unenviable task but one he carried out with respect and decorum.

From those who survived the Second World War, just as in the previous world conflict, a suitable memorial was sought to honour the lost musicians and buglers. With voluntary donations from comrades still serving, a set of fourteen silver fanfare trumpets was commissioned, with the names of the ships in which they were lost inscribed inside the bell of the instruments. The commissioning written charter, in keeping with their inception, states that the trumpets shall be styled as 'The Memorial Silver Trumpets of the Royal Marines School of Music' and this title shall on no occasion be abbreviated.

During the Second World War, the Royal Navy lost 278 major warships as well over 1,000 smaller vessels, so it is easy to see how amongst the many thousands of sailors that were lost there was a large number of band members who never returned. The total loss of musicians and buglers in ships during the war was 225, which was a high percentage of the Band Service numbers of that time. The deaths of these men along with their musical talent would have left a huge hole in the service and it must have taken a long while for them to recover to their pre-war strength, which, while noteworthy, is of course insignificant compared to the loss and grief of their families.

As well as those sailors, Marines and musicians who were lost, many thousands more became survivors of ships that were sunk. Although surviving a sinking was preferable to going down with your ship, it left you with very few personal effects and probably only the clothes you were stood up in. Imagine then having acquired new documents, including ID cards, and personal items only to be sunk and to survive again. One such unfortunate was RM musician Morris Colbourne who, as a member of a ship's band, was sunk twice but lived to tell the tale. Such was his extraordinary survival story that later in his life a TV crew visited him in a retirement home. In the

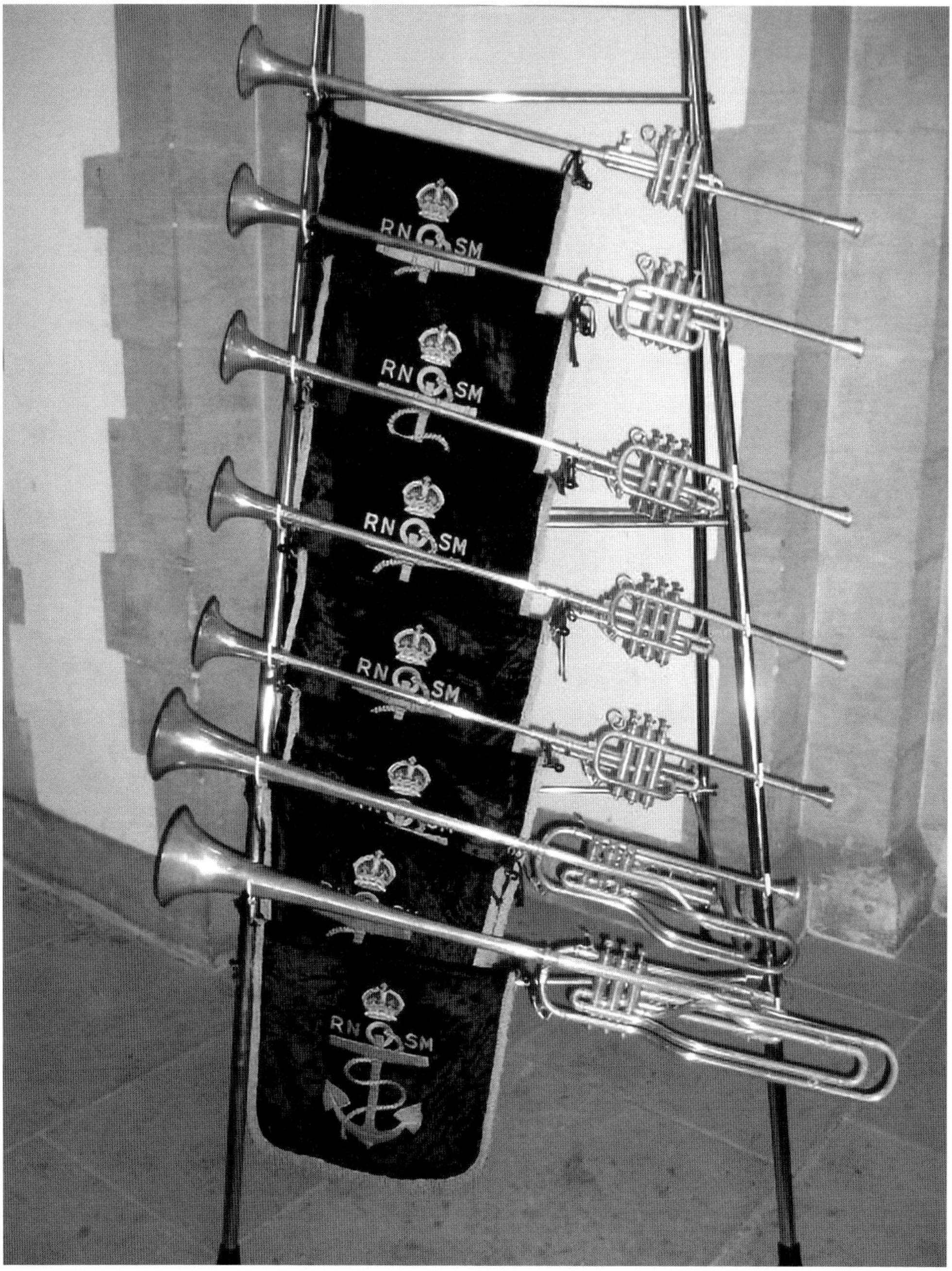

The Memorial Silver Trumpets of the Royal Marines School of Music, commemorating those musicians who lost their lives aboard ships in the Second World War.

home, Morris was one of only a few gentlemen amongst a large number of female residents, so consequently, he was quite popular in the common room. Nearing the end of the recording, the interviewer commented on Morris's remarkable story and his age of 84. At this point, Morris told the TV crew they must not broadcast the interview as his girlfriends in the home thought he was only 74!

Another notable story to come out of the Second World War involving a ship's band involved the cruiser HMS *Trinidad*. While protecting Russian convoys the ship fired several of her own torpedoes during an attack but due to a faulty gyro, one of the torpedoes circled back and hit the ship. It struck near the Royal Marines mess and killed thirty-two of her crew. One of the musicians who survived was RM band musician George Lloyd, who vividly recalled being the last one through a lower hatch before it was slammed shut, thereby both physically sealing the hatch and the fate of the people trapped below it. The reason I include George Lloyd's story amongst the many thousands of life-and-death instances, is that he went on to become a well-known British composer, comparable with the likes of Benjamin Britten and Edward Elgar. Now, in more enlightened times, it is easier to understand how such a traumatic event might affect an individual, but back then there was little understanding or, I daresay, sympathy. That hatch slamming down on his shipmates had a profound effect on George, leaving him with what we would now call post-traumatic stress disorder (PTSD). The change in him was dramatic and the events coloured his moods, and this was later evident in his deep and thoughtful musical compositions.

A final note about the unlucky ship HMS *Trinidad*. Having torpedoed herself, she limped into Murmansk harbour for initial repairs but once she sailed for home, she was again attacked by German bombers. The encounter was devastating, killing another sixty-three men, including twenty survivors from another sunken ship that were being taken home. With the *Trinidad* deemed not to be salvageable, the remaining crew were taken off and she was eventually sunk by one of our own ships, becoming a permanent war grave.

To put one face to help represent those musicians of the Second World War and the many hundreds who were lost, I have included here a photograph showing ship survivor Band Corporal Horace George Vincent. In the picture, Horace and other band members look happy and no doubt greatly relieved to have survived and been rescued from a sinking ship. Sadly, a few short months after this picture was taken, Horace and other band members would be lost in the sinking of HMS *Hermione*. As well as the obvious family sadness, there is added poignancy as Horace died not knowing that at home, his wife had given birth to a baby boy. Another name, memorial and a family's future changed forever.

It seems that through the millennia, every country that goes to war, regardless of their religion, has a belief that *their* god is on *their* side. There are some obvious motivational reasons for this and it can help justify or rationalise the taking of life. It goes some way to encourage the fighting man and can provide some small comfort for those he may leave behind. As well as general prayers, most armed forces have their own dedicated prayer, and although I am not an overly religious

Horace Vincent (third from left), having been sunk and rescued, with his fellow bandmate survivors.

person myself, there is still something in the Royal Marines Band Service prayer that resonates with me. Even without the religious connotation, it says something about how music can bring joy and inspiration, so I will include it here for you to make you own mind up on interpretation and its meaning. However you choose to read it, I think it an appropriate inclusion here, and a gentle and suitable ending to this chapter.

Almighty and eternal Lord God,
in whose sight and love
live our memories of many generations
of those who have served you
in the Band Service of the Royal Marines:
we thank you for the rich heritage
of the music placed in our hands,
and for the joy and inspiration
it brings to men.
Enable us with our whole heart to serve you,
that by your grace
and through our gift of music,
we may continue to inspire,
help and lead men.
We ask these things
in the name of Jesus Christ our Lord.
Amen.

The Reverend Lovell Pocock

Chapter Four

Aircraft Carrier Deployments

As the Royal Marines Band Service provides the bulk of the music for the Royal Navy, it of course follows that many of its musicians will have found themselves at sea during their careers, to which their service and losses pay testament during the world wars. I say the bulk of the music because there are volunteer bands at many of the Royal Navy shore establishments and on some ships. These are composed of officers and sailors who have previous experience of playing an instrument or want to learn one. On detached duty from the Royal Marines Band Service, a musically talented SNCO (senior/staff non-commissioned officer) is sent to teach and conduct these volunteer bands. Of course, all RMBS musicians are musically talented, but it requires a certain confidence to take on, teach and conduct amateur musicians, and to get them to a decent standard to play in public or in a ship's wardroom. Usually, a band sergeant or above wanting the conducting or unique experience is sent, but sometimes drafting needs outweigh personal choice and a suitable candidate is wrenched from a cosy band position to go forth. I can say I have never met anyone who did not enjoy the experience of being 'the boss' of their own little band, which not only provided a good standard of music, but also an outlet for any musical talent residing within the Royal Navy. The navy gave up their own school of music in 1950, handing over the requirement of full-time musical training and provision of music to the Royal Marines, which given the spectacular result, was probably a good idea!

After the Second World War, even though the peacetime fleet was diminishing, there were plenty of warships and aircraft carriers that still required the services of a ship-sized band. Depending on the ship, the average size of an aircraft carrier band was around twenty in number, which gave enough musical combinations for a marching band, concert band, a small wardroom orchestra and perhaps surprisingly (or perhaps not) on a Royal Navy ship, a dance band. The Royal Navy was still something of a world leader in naval aviation in this era, and with aircraft carriers able to impress and project political power around the world, they were still deemed important by the government and the Admiralty. In the 1960s, the UK still had eight aircraft carriers, which was good for the naval budget, but having these huge assets sitting in a dockyard was not cost-effective, so ships of this time frequently went on long commissions around the world to literally and figuratively 'fly the flag'.

HMS *Centaur* leaving Portsmouth for a lengthy and eventful commission.

Having sailed from Portsmouth in 1963, the aircraft carrier HMS *Centaur*, on her forth commission, found herself setting out on one such lengthy deployment. Heading to the Far East, the ship, her crew and RM band found themselves involved in several notable incidents and conflicts, in which the band members were to play an important part. Even as she sailed out of Portsmouth for this long period, including Christmas away from home and family, the already dull mood took on a more sombre note set by the captain's announcement that US President J.F. Kennedy had been assassinated. This added another nuance to the world's political situation of the day and made the future just a little more uncertain. Having played the ship out of port, one musician recorded in his diary, 'So we sailed away, for a year and a day,' reflecting the already heavy mood on the ship.

Things could only get better, they thought, but unbeknownst to the *Centaur*'s crew and band, they would have an eventful voyage, finding themselves involved in the rescue mission of the TSMS *Lakonia*, as well as in the Dar Mutiny in Africa, and then, for good measure, in the Indonesian–Malaysian confrontation – quite a trip for a peacetime commission.

One of the youngest musicians aboard was John Ware, who would end his career at the top of the Band Service hierarchy as Lieutenant Colonel John Ware,

Principal Director of Music Royal Marines. Serving for thirty-four years, amongst his many career highlights was as officer in charge of Stonehouse band when they deployed on the *Canberra* for Operation Corporate in The Falklands. I am grateful to John for providing me with his notes for the main details of this chapter. I was also delighted to find Richard Baker, another stalwart of the Band Service of that era, living close to me in Deal, and so am grateful to him for his memories and added colour to the stories. Richard's service began in 1956, which might seem a long time ago, because it is. His full career in the RMBS saw him achieve the rank of colour sergeant, before leaving the Royal Marines to teach music to the Oman Navy. Richard's contribution to the Band Service of his era is held in high regard, as was his good humour and wit, as well as his uncanny ability to look good in a dress (I should add, while taking part in a charity panto!). Both Richard and John's notes, along with those of Tony Platts, add background detail and emotion to their interesting stories.

HMS *Centaur* was steaming in a bit of a hurry as she had to rendezvous with another aircraft carrier, HMS *Ark Royal*, to relieve her from her station, 'east of Suez'. Ploughing heavily through the Bay of Biscay, even the large carrier was rolling through the heavy sea, causing the new boys (girls on ships would not happen for another thirty years) to reconsider their career choice and their last full meal. Things and stomachs took a turn for the better when she eventually 'rounded the corner' and found calmer waters, but just as she was about to enter the Strait of Gibraltar, an event happening several hundred miles to the west caused a major change of course.

Overnight on 22 December, several distress calls were received from the cruise liner TSMS *Lakonia*, on fire near the island of Madeira. Having made good progress, *Centaur* arrived on Christmas Eve and in the early morning light could clearly see that the *Lakonia* was ablaze and an evacuation was taking place. One officer described the scene as 'shambolic' as they witnessed some of the lifeboats being launched and people already in the water wearing lifejackets. The *Centaur*'s captain ordered the ship's cutter away to search for survivors and this was manned by an officer, a stoker, a coxswain and two medics. The medics were actually two young members of the ship's Royal Marines band, musicians Richard Baker and Willi Watson. The notional title of 'medic' was bestowed upon them after a short pre-deployment medic course at Lympstone, with Willi Watson recording that this mostly consisted of carrying each other around on stretchers and applying bandages to imaginary wounds.

With the cutter pitching in the swell, they arrived at the first of what they hoped were survivors. The two musicians grabbed at the life vest and pulling the person on board found them to be heavier than expected, which was because they had

The TSMS *Lakonia* was already in a distressed state when HMS *Centaur* arrived on scene to assist in the rescue operation.

already drowned and were full of seawater. The shock of suddenly having to deal with the dead was made worse when hauling them aboard caused air to pass the vocal chords and they appeared to groan. The same thing was repeated several times over as they recovered more bodies of men, women and children. Hoping they had done their duty and could now return to their ship, the cutter was then tasked to go alongside a civilian tanker and take on more recovered bodies. This did not go well as one body was so badly damaged that during the transfer, the tarpaulin tipped, covering the cutter crew in seawater, blood and body parts. Not for the first time that day, the two musicians looked at each other and shrugged, but there was still more macabre work to be done and dark duty to fulfil. Their final task was to lighten the cutter so it could be hauled back aboard, so both musicians, already tired from their efforts, were told to haul themselves up a skinny rope ladder to the deck. Surprised at the silent reception from the sailors, they realised why when everyone was looking back down into the cutter and could see the strewn lifeless bodies of the men, women and children, no doubt relating them to their families back home. Another ship's cutter was then launched and band members Corporal Willi Shears and Musician Roger Smith took up the mantle until eventually, seventy-eight bodies had been recovered – a good portion of the final tally of 128 dead. Musician Tony Platts remembered the bodies laid out on the flight deck and one of the older, wiser crewmembers saying, 'Don't worry, bandy, you will not harm them; look upon them like waxwork figures.' This was not to dehumanise them in any way, but advice to get the job done with reverence and respect.

On completion of their sad task and back in the band mess aboard, Richard Baker, in typical 'gallows humour' that is sometimes needed to deal with such situations, said laconically, 'What a way to spend Christmas.' The reward for their arduous duty was a double tot of rum, the tot being a daily ration on Royal Navy ships of that time … but I like to think you knew that already. It is worth recording that Willi Watson was a French horn player and Richard Baker a euphonium and cello player. With the ship still in sombre mood, the next day's unloading of the dead meant for a muted Christmas celebration, until the band once again returned to their musical role and managed to lift the ship's company's spirits a little. It is hard to imagine Richard's talented fingers returning to playing his cello after the horrible ordeal they had been put through in the cold Atlantic waters. Richard recalls the ship's doctor examining some of the bodies for life and needlessly stating, 'This one only has half a head, so I pronounce him dead,' which seemed a little unnecessary to Richard at the time.

As if the start of HMS *Centaur*'s long commission had not been memorable enough, a few short weeks later they would be called upon to assist in quelling a mutiny. Remembering this is 'old school' politics and gunboat diplomacy, I find myself amazed to be writing about revolution and mutiny with information from those who were actually there. Following on from the Zanzibar Revolution in January 1964, a regiment called the Tanganyika Rifles decided the time was right for them to mutiny, relieve their officers of their authority and seize key points in Dar es Salaam. A throwback to colonial days, the regiment still had a high proportion of British officers serving in the regiment. The government decided that the UK would intervene and put this part of the world to rights. Once again, HMS *Centaur* was in the right place at the wrong time and she was tasked with assisting in the operation by transporting and inserting members of 45 Commando Royal Marines to quell the uprising. What came as yet another surprise to the band on *Centaur* was that someone decided that the band would 'go in' with the Commandos, and march through the town. Perhaps this was a show of strength and confidence to assert dominance … or maybe just an officer having had too much gin with his lunch. Whatever the reason, the operation was a great success, as within twenty-four hours, the mutineers had surrendered, been disarmed and the regiment disbanded. Some of the band members were then returned to medic duties, greeting the arriving Belvedere helicopters that were bringing some of the wounded mutineers aboard for medical treatment. The Belvedere helicopter was a twin-rotor design, which might make the reader think of the more modern Chinook; but emanating from a 1950s design, the Belvedere was nowhere near as powerful or capable. Amongst its many idiosyncrasies and design faults was one where the upward-opening door could be slammed down shut onto the unwary passenger or stretcher-bearer by the rotor downwash. Flight decks are dangerous places at the best of times, but being eaten by a helicopter door added a certain uncertainty to your day. The helicopter did eventually have a redesign and the doors were changed to more useful and less dangerous sliding versions.

John Ware recalls the surreal situation of the band setting up and playing in the town square while armed Royal Marines Commandos rounded up the stragglers from the mutiny. Whether it was the threat of armed intervention by our Marines, or the sound of a twenty-piece ship's band playing the 'Colonel Bogey March' that brought down the mutiny is not recorded, but I think 45 Commando probably have the bragging rights to this one.

The band's march through Dar es Salaam the following day was greeted with great delight by many of the residents, and on completion they were invited to the local Gymkhana Club for drinks with the expat community. While enjoying the hospitality afforded them, the weather in the bay took a turn for the worse and the small boats could not make the return journey to their ship, anchored way out in the bay. Now temporarily stranded, to make the best of a good situation, festivities continued and beds were found with the local police superintendent. The next day,

HMS *Centaur*'s band flying the flag in Dar es Salaam.

Wounded mutineers arriving by Belvedere helicopter.

with the weather improved, the band thanked their hosts kindly and made their way back aboard the *Centaur*, which having now successfully quelled a mutiny, up-anchored and set sail for Singapore. Like it or not, this was gunboat diplomacy of its time, albeit using an aircraft carrier, a Commando unit and a Royal Marines band.

As well as being 'on station', one of the main reasons for HMS *Centaur*'s Far East deployment was due to the rise in tensions between Indonesia and the new Federation of Malaysia. The federation at that time included Singapore, but this provoked threats, infiltrations and incursions by the Indonesian forces across the Malacca Strait from Sumatra. Such was the importance of protecting British interests in the Far East region, it was deemed necessary to have two aircraft carriers on station, along with other attendant warships and support vessels. Having passed, saluted and relieved HMS *Ark Royal*, which having finished her commission headed home, HMS *Centaur* took up station, taking it in turns to patrol the Malacca Strait with another British aircraft carrier, HMS *Victorious*. It is worth noting that all three of the carriers named above would have had their own ship-sized band. In 1976, I would find myself serving aboard HMS *Ark Royal* – of course, in her band.

On HMS *Centaur* and *Victorious*, operational tensions were running high as the Indonesian head of state, President Sukarno, had taken umbrage at British ships

Ranks of 45 Commando RM sleeping rough in the ship's hangar.

patrolling 'his waters' and thwarting his political and military aims. He issued many and various thinly veiled threats, including the use of a submarine attack against the British fleet. Consequently, the crew and band on *Centaur* were in a constant state of readiness and alert. The carrier's readiness state included two Royal Navy Sea Vixen aircraft ranged on the deck ready for a quick reaction take-off in less than two minutes. Although supported by other vessels, *Centaur*'s main defence was her aircraft, including early warning aircraft (AEW), so her proud boast that nothing could get close enough that would need to be engaged by her rather outdated and short-range Bofors guns kept nerves to a minimum. That was until on one occasion when John reports an urgent announcement over the ship's Tannoy: 'Unidentified aircraft approaching the ship!' Seconds later, a jet swooped over the deck at a height of 50 feet (15 metres). Braced for the worst, it came as a great relief to hear a second, less tense, pipe over the Tannoy: 'It's okay, it's one of ours.'

Looking back on these incidents, it seems as if the band on HMS *Centaur* had more than their fair share of excitement and sadness for what should have been a peacetime Far East commission and port visits in exotic places. As Director of Music of the Plymouth band on *Canberra* during the Falklands War, John Ware would have further cause to worry about enemy aircraft, but on that occasion his concerns would be substantiated and the danger real.

Ship's musician Richard Baker's final memory on this part of the deployment was the band being told they were required to play for an important dinner in Singapore, and so would be temporarily leaving HMS *Centaur* to be transferred to another ship for the onward journey to the island. Having assembled all their kit, uniforms and instruments, the band were horrified to find that no helicopters were available, so they were each going to be transferred across to a Royal Fleet Auxiliary ship by jackstay. This method involves a line being passed between two ships on which a small wooden seat is pulled back and forth by a team of sailors on each end, transferring the unfortunate passenger across the gap over the sea. No matter what the weather, a raging chasm was guaranteed due to the proximity of the two ships ploughing through the water only 30 or 40 metres apart, their combined wakes crashing together midstream. This method has been used extensively to transfer personnel and stores if urgently required, but to a man, the band felt this was not urgent enough to warrant the risky transfer across the chasm and the potential loss to life, limb or trumpet; but the 'exigencies of the service' were once again played like a trump card, and the decision and 'mission impossible' transfer confirmed.

With Royal Fleet Auxiliary (RFA) ship *Tidesurge* on station 100 feet away, each of the band was unceremoniously transferred across the maelstrom of surging sea to the RFA, each surprised to have made it without incident or wet feet. Due to the inherent risks associated with jackstay transfers, the procedure always commanded an audience of 'goofers', who with nothing better to do would be secretly hoping to see some stores lost, or some poor unfortunate officer inadvertently dunked by a slack line. On this day there was an added spice to the transfer as HMS *Centaur*'s well-known band were again providing the entertainment, but in a very different way as they risked everything they owned cross-decking to the other ship. Amongst the watching and grinning goofers, Richard Baker clearly remembers seeing a sailor cheerily waving to him when he was midway between the two ships, but clinging onto the rope dearly for life, he chose not to wave back.

With post-war carrier operations and deployments still deemed necessary to project some influence around the globe, as well as to protect the dwindling interests of former colonial countries, there was a steady stream of Far East commissions for those who wanted them, and sometimes for those who did not. One of the ships that came up in my research was another aircraft carrier, HMS *Eagle*. Like all ships of her time, the *Eagle* carried her own Royal Marines band, the members of which, just like their predecessors on HMS *Centaur*, would find themselves having a more interesting and exciting cruise than they might have imagined.

Rather than the usual routine of a rolling programme of drafting musicians in and out of the band, for unknown reasons, HMS *Eagle*'s band was formed up separately at the Royal Marines School of Music at Deal, under the experienced eye of Royal Marines Bandmaster Gilbert 'Jock' Brown. My main source for this section was one

A typical jackstay transfer between two ships.

of the young buglers drafted into the band, Christopher Archer. Much later in his career, Chris would become a warrant officer and was one of the most well-liked and respected drum majors of his generation – able to both command respect and still get the job done, with either serious admonishment of a mistake or an appropriate funny comment. There is also the mystery as to why some of his contemporaries call Chris 'Dan', which I am also guilty of without knowing the reason. (STOP PRESS: An explanation from Chris arrived late in the book writing process. The BBC radio show called *The Archers* had a character called Dan Archer, and so, like many nicknames in the services, the name stuck. It could have been much worse as there was another character in the show called Doris Archer, and it would not have taken much for Chris to have been awarded that name for a lifetime!)

Having been issued his musicians, Bandmaster Gilbert Brown formed the band and got them playing musically to his standard before they undertook what was then called 'pre-embarkation training'. By all accounts, life was good for a young bugler at that time, and so with the training complete, Dan and the rest of the ship's band joined HMS *Eagle* in Plymouth. In June, they sailed for a Far East commission, which was music to the ears of many of the young members of the band because the Far East was where all the fun was – and I do mean *all the fun*!

Apart from the fun and 'good runs ashore' (a run ashore is what sailors and marines do when leaving a ship or barracks for a night out), the official mission and reason for exporting 2,500 testosterone-fuelled sailors and Marines to the Orient was to relieve HMS *Hermes*, which had been on station and due to return home. The band's main role aboard a strike carrier was mainly entertainment and ceremonial, but *Eagle*'s band also had a role manning the aircraft tracking stations for the ship's guns and missiles. Turning south, as nearly all Royal Navy ships did, *Eagle* would normally have sailed through the Mediterranean and taken the shortcut through the Suez Canal, but the Arab–Israeli Six-Day War had blocked the canal and so she was routed down the Atlantic via Ascension Island. This did allow them the bonus of a run ashore in Cape Town before rounding the Cape of Good Hope and her onward voyage to the east.

It was at this point in Britain's history that a Royal Marines band would once again become involved in military action, in this case, the band of HMS *Eagle*. With political and local unrest in the former colony of Aden, or South Yemen, as it is now called, after 129 years of British rule it was decided that British troops would be withdrawn. The band serving aboard HMS *Eagle* found themselves front and centre when the rather hurried, and some might say untidy, withdrawal from Aden took place.

As I am fond of stating, usually by way of an excuse, I am not a historian, but a potted history for some background might be useful. Due to its strategic location rather than its commercial value, Aden had been under British control for over a hundred years, which by acknowledging that colonialism was *of its time* and not something we can change by wishing it away, you will have to accept that's just how things were. The rights and wrong of that occupation and colonialism can be debated until the bovines come home, but do it in your own time and in your own way. Rebellion, civil unrest, terrorism and the general withdrawing of British troops from previous colonies around the world added to the tensions and pressure to pull out. Terrorist acts against the military, their families and other civilians also added weight to the government's decision to leave Aden, and so an accelerated withdrawal plan was put into place, but a plan that gathered momentum as the end date approached. While HMS *Eagle* was on passage to Singapore, the withdrawal plan had reached a crisis point, and so she found herself diverted to Aden so that her aircraft could fly missions in support of the beleaguered British troops. This part of the operation took place over several weeks, and with the worsening political and military situation becoming desperate, it was decided to fly in the band from HMS *Eagle*. However, flown ashore into RAF Khormaskar, the band were not given any military tasks as Royal Marines from 42 Commando and 45 Commando were firmly holding the line and maintaining order of sorts in the quickly deteriorating situation. There were undoubtedly many army and RAF personnel also involved in Aden, and apologies for nothing other than this scant acknowledgement of their service in this difficult theatre of operations.

With the big hand of the withdrawal clock seemingly spinning ever faster, a day arrived when it was decided nothing could quell an angry mob like a Royal Marines band, so the band were quickly driven into the town square, where they set up to play for the final taking down of the British flag. With chaos and danger all around them, and a sense of timing and humour, Bandmaster Gilbert Brown decided to play a tune called 'Things Ain't What They Used to Be', the irony of which was lost on the Arabs but enjoyed by some of the musically educated Marines. Having been detailed off to look after the band's security while they were playing, the RM Commandos appeared to have two oft-repeated maxims: first, 'Watch your back' and secondly, 'Leave no beer for the Arabs', which by Dan Archer's account was an order they successfully fulfilled.

By most descriptions from those who were there, the withdrawal was hurried and dangerous, and accompanied by some very quick tempo playing of the 'Colonel Bogey March' at a speed that would have both surprised and horrified composer Kenneth Alford. With few people having the time or inclination to photograph the orderly withdrawal or hurried evacuation of Aden, whichever version of events you prefer, it seems to have been captured well in a cartoon of the time.

"All right lads, the usual routine—half a dozen bars of the old 'Retreat,' haul down the flag, and beat it back to the beach. We'll skip the 'slow march' bit today 'cos we're a bit pressed for time. . . !"

A *Navy News* cartoon of its time aptly captures the 'music surrounded by chaos' moment of the Aden withdrawal.

After the excitement of the Aden exit, HMS *Eagle* was released to continue her planned Far East commission and she eventually made it to Singapore for Christmas. She also made some memorable port visits to Freemantle in Western Australia, the Philippines and Hong Kong, before being recalled to Aden to assist for a second time. Although the British rule had ended and control passed back to the indigenous people, internal factions were still fighting and it was thought the remaining British civilians might need evacuating, so HMS *Eagle* and HMS *Bulwark*, which had 40 Commando embarked, were stood by off the coast. Here ends the short but memorable contribution the Royal Marines ship's band of HMS *Eagle* made to the Aden withdrawal. Evacuations from Aden will feature again later in this book.

In the 1970s, although the direction of naval air power was changing and the cost of keeping a fleet of aircraft carriers at sea was taking ever bigger bites out of the defence budget, when I joined the Royal Marines in 1973, the British fleet was still firing fighter jets from the decks of ships with steam catapults. I was pleased to hear this because as a young boy living at Mountwise, near Devonport Dockyard, I had seen many aircraft carriers sail out of Plymouth, their decks lined with exciting planes and helicopters, with the added sound of a Royal Marines band reaching the shore as they played the ship out. The combination was a heady one to any young boy stood watching these huge ships cruising past just a hundred meters from Mutton Cove. It certainly made an impression on me and, along with my father's death serving in 42 Commando, almost certainly played a subliminal part in my career choice.

My own sea time on an aircraft carrier came very early in my career, in fact, just as soon as I was deemed fit for adult service and released into the wild from the Royal Marines School of Music. HMS *Ark Royal* was what I would describe as a *real* aircraft carrier, one with steam catapults that threw jets into the air and caught them again on arrester wires when they had enough of flying and came home for

HMS *Ark Royal* in 1976, arriving in the USA for Bicentennial celebrations of the memorable kind.

Chapter Five

Humanitarian Deployments

Not all RMBS deployments have involved arming musicians for military duties, or even giving them medical type duties; those we will be delving into in later chapters. I thought it would make more interesting reading to start with the understated softer commissions and exercises before moving on to the harder and grittier military missions, but even some of these softer deployments might surprise you and raise an eyebrow.

In peacetime, due to the nature of some of their training, sometimes the Royal Marines Band ranks are handpicked for certain roles within deployments – in particular, where perhaps a more thoughtful approach is needed. Of course, I am not suggesting the Royal Marine green beret Commando is not thoughtful, considerate and where needed compassionate, but shall I just say *horses for courses* and swiftly move on before I offend anyone who has yet to grasp my sense of humour. There will also be financial and practical reasons why a musician in a military band might be the preferred option, as in these days of overall reduced manpower it can be cost-effective to use all available resources, and that occasionally means involving the RMBS.

Having been 'there' myself (wherever *there* is) on many occasions, I cannot help feel that there are also a few quite savvy senior officers who realise that as well as getting some quality polished boots on the ground to assist in their operation, they are also the temporary custodians of a group of highly talented musicians. Having them play after working hours never fails to impress in theatre; it is handy for mess dinners and also helps to entertain off-duty personnel. Most of the military band deployments in theatre have involved playing for a mess dinner, of some sort, some of which have been in unusual locations.

On the other side of the planning coin, ad hoc or even planned deployments do play havoc with the RMBS's own work and music commitments, but with these deployment decisions taken at a very senior level, and no doubt for good reasons, the band management system just has to adapt, smile, and send the manpower on request – or, as the military call it, 'as ordered'. There are some examples of operations in this book that decimated the planned music programmes of several of the bands, and in one instance, all of the Band Service commitments for the most

Former musician and lifelong trombone player Dave Thornber, being treated by serving members of the RMBS during the Covid pandemic of 2020–21.

part of a year; but it is never forgotten that the Band Service is part of the Royal Marines Corps first, and must act accordingly.

At the time of writing, the most recent request for manpower assistance came during the 2021 Covid crisis, where the UK was sometimes in lockdown, sometimes not, depending on which government broadcast you watched or which government minister was reading it. With the bulk of the population wanting and needing inoculation against the virus, the National Health Service was overwhelmed, not least because many of its own doctors and nurses were infected and then had to stay away from their place of work. This might sound obvious now, but in ten years' time, someone picking this up in a charity shop might not know what we went through during the Covid lockdowns!

Because of manpower demands, many branches of the military were called upon to support the NHS at this difficult time, including members of the RMBS. It did not take much in the way of additional medical training to get band members up to speed and capable of delivering injections. Sent to various medical centres and hospitals around the country, their work and their attitude towards the task was gratefully received by those with whom they came into contact. One of their patients who was particularly pleased to see their Royal Marines Band Service shoulder flashes was former RMBS trombonist David Thornber, who having appeared at his local hospital for his Covid jab, was happy to bare his arm for a talented flute player to inject him! The assistance of the RMBS during this national crisis was much appreciated by the NHS and is just another example of the flexibility of the RMBS in times of need.

As well as assisting on the home front, the following three chapters represent the wide range of humanitarian help given to various communities and countries abroad when they were in need. They range from assisting locals after a hurricane, to Her Majesty's Royal Yacht *Britannia* having to become a refugee rescue vessel. For the full story, read on …

Chapter Six

Africa: Operation Gritrock

In October 2014, members of the Royal Marines Band in Scotland were sent on detached duty and deployed on Operation Gritrock aboard RFA *Argus*. The deployment was in response to the Ebola virus outbreak on the African continent. The UK government decided that some urgent medical assistance from all three services and members of the Royal Marines Band Service were needed to help the local medical services contain the virus and prevent further spreading of the disease. Under Operation Gritrock, and sub-mission heading of 'Assisting in the Joint Area of Operations', thirteen members of the RMBS were deployed under

HMS *Argus* at sea.

the leadership of Bandmaster WO2 Ross Hunt. His tenure lasted until January 2015, when he was relieved by Bandmaster WO2 David Prentice, who was my main source of information for this chapter. An interesting side note (at least to some) is that when I was the percussion instructor at the Royal Marines School of Music in Deal, David Prentice was one of my drumming students. Despite that, he went on to have a stellar career in the Band Service, finishing his time as a Bandmaster WO1, and the bandmaster in Plymouth band.

The six-month deployment of musicians was no mean feat given the relatively small size of Scotland band and the gaps left in it by these temporarily *stolen* performers. This led to various instrument categories being temporarily loaned, people doubling up on instruments, and the band structure reorganised to cover the deployed ranks. On board RFA *Argus*, living conditions were reported as being 'pretty good', all things considered, as indeed they are on most RFA vessels compared to Royal Navy warships. This is, of course, subjective and dependent upon your rank and in which part of the ship you are billeted.

Their work both on board and ashore was unofficially titled 'donners and doffers', which was described by David Prentice thus:

> Due to the RM Band ranks' diligence to adhere to instructions, and being slightly more demonstrative compared to RN ranks, we were tasked with ensuring everyone who came on board and went ashore went through exactly the same extremely strict donning and doffing of the personal protective equipment. The PPE was essential for your own protection and required to work in the joint area of operations ashore – in the heart of the Ebola crisis and in the villages.

I think we can take from that, and from those who know Dave Prentice, that they took no nonsense and sensibly applied the rules as they should in order to avoid infection.

The importance of strict control and wearing of PPE could not be overstated given the virulence of the Ebola virus itself. To be able to help others, first you must protect yourself, and given that the Ebola virus had a death rate of up to 90 per cent, with about 12,000 deaths locally, any infection making it aboard the ship environment could have been disastrous. In regards to that duty, it seems the band members did a very good job and only one case made it aboard the ship, but that was not down to any lack of diligence on their part. Unfortunately, there was one case of a British nurse being infected, which was put down to either very bad luck, contaminated equipment or possibly a mistake in their own self-cleansing regime, but luckily, in this case, it proved to be non-fatal.

The band members also found themselves ashore helping to operate at landing sites where casualties needed loading or unloading from the helicopters. Working around helicopters that are still 'turning and burning' requires another skill set, or at least a greater awareness of the dangers presented by the whirling chopper blades. Even approaching a helicopter from the wrong direction without the pilot seeing you or straying towards the dangerous tail rotor area can be deadly, needing extra eyes and ears to mitigate the risks – risks that were greatly increased due to a lack of radio communications. In time-honoured fashion, the band members quickly adapted and learnt the correct hand signals to communicate with the pilots and crew, which hastened the task and lessened the risks to all concerned.

As with nearly all RMBS deployments, there was enough musical talent to form various small combinations to play around the ship. Not only was this important for the ship's morale, it was also important to the band members to keep up their core skills for later reintegration into the musical fold. From the small pool of just thirteen musicians, they were able to field a small marching band, a quintet, a function band and a Dixieland jazz band – but not all at the same time!

There were many funny dits to come out of this deployment but the one that first comes to David Prentice's mind is when he was invited to the petty officers' mess for a drink. It seemed that the traditional game of Uckers (for the uninitiated, think of the board game Ludo but with very different navy rules) had taken second place to a game where the simple aim was to don a tattered boxing glove and punch the person sitting next to you!

Not every deployment or commission starts with fireworks or ends with a fanfare, but sometimes it is just a record of the RMBS quietly and efficiently getting on with the task in hand. It is good to see, though, that their work ethic and contribution to the successful operation, both on and off duty, was noted by senior officers, with several letters of thanks and commendation sent to the Band Service hierarchy.

Dave Prentice returned with memories of a job well done and a hand-carved African souvenir.

Chapter Seven

Operation Tellar

In September 1998, the Band of HM Royal Marines Flag Officer Scotland and Northern Ireland (FOSNI) were looking forward to 'a nice little jolly' aboard the newly commissioned Royal Navy ship HMS *Ocean*. The ship, looking all the world like an aircraft carrier, was actually designated a 'landing platform helicopter' and designed from the hull up to support amphibious operations. In this, her first major outing, *Ocean* was undertaking a tour around the Caribbean, heading for such exotic ports such as Tortola, Nassau and Curaçao. WO1 Bandmaster James Parkinson, who was then a young musician in the band, provided details about this trip.

The grand tour started well in Tortola, with little to report except that a sailor fell between the jetty and the liberty boat taking him back to the ship. It seems that

HMS *Ocean*, with an array of helicopters on deck.

just like toast always falling butter side down, whenever a sailor falls off a liberty boat it is, for some reason, always on the way back to the ship after sampling local beverages; but no matter what the reason for the fall and unplanned uniform wash, he was safely recovered.

James records that nearly all the band had a good 'run ashore' in Tortola, with the exception of fellow percussionist Tom 'Jock' Scade, who decided to stay aboard and save his money for the other ports. The ship sailed and the band set about rehearsing for the long list of forthcoming musical engagements around the Caribbean. Unfortunately, due to the sudden arrival of tropical storm Mitch into the Western Caribbean, Jock Scade would not have a chance to spend his hard-earned groats in the port of Nassau.

Here I need to detail a few facts about this very aggressive storm, given the name Mitch by weather forecasters, which had begun its life way out in the Atlantic. Once it had gathered momentum and strength, Hurricane Mitch raged in from the Atlantic into the Caribbean, becoming the second deadliest hurricane on record. Striking the South American coastline, its strength and slow movement across the ground caused massive flooding, resulting in the deaths of around 12,000 people in coastal Honduras and Nicaragua. With winds recorded at 180mph, it peaked at Category 5, which is at the top of the hurricane scale. In the age of satellite communication, the outside world quickly knew the scale of the death and destruction and the international community soon started to put a relief plan into operation. The Americans led the way, and the relatively local Mexican government was also quick to act. The British government were keen to help, and required HMS *Ocean* to change course and redeploy under the now operational name of Operation Tellar.

With the ship now performing in a real life-and-death scenario, the band were tasked with various working parties to prepare for casualties and to deploy boats and landing craft to look out for survivors. One of the ship's lookouts luckily spotted some capsised fishing boats with the survivors clinging desperately to the wreckage. Once the dehydrated fishermen were aboard, they were looked after in the ship's sickbay by the medical staff and some of the band. Once HMS *Ocean* reached the coast of Nicaragua, the fishermen were loaded into landing craft and with some of the band acting as escorts, they were returned to their home port to their very grateful families. So pleased were the locals to see that the Royal Navy and Royal Marines were there to help that they produced, among other things, many fresh lobsters for them to take back on board the ship for dinner. Whether it was the prospect of lobster for dinner, or the excitement of not yet having spent any money, Jock Scade almost made it back to the ship in the landing craft when, without warning, he found himself vomiting over the shoes of the Royal Marines colour sergeant in charge of the landing craft! I expect an apology was offered and kindly words exchanged between the errant musician and the colour sergeant, but with experience telling us that the words were probably in one direction more than the other.

Several other members of FOSNI band had better sea legs, and had acquired in their careers their powerboat licences, enabling them to drive various inshore motorboats. Brian Lloyd, a versatile musician, pianist and singer, was one of the motorboat drivers and vividly recalls the trips ashore. Loaded with equipment, supplies, water and rice, they headed up into the smaller rivers and tributaries delivering their aid and working parties, helping the locals wherever they could. Their presence brought comfort, and the help they gave was appreciated greatly by the local population, whilst also widening the reputation of the United Kingdom Royal Navy and Royal Marines as a force for good. Although working hard and doing a good thing, one of Brian's abiding memories concerned the local wildlife. As they were sleeping outdoors in the open, appreciative of their fresh blood were the local mosquito population, who feasted on the fresh-faced musicians, leaving them with hundreds of mozzie bites and the accompanying scratching. The only consolation (if fresh lobster in exchange for incessant itching is a consolation) was that some of the many lobsters did make it to the ship's galley and were prepared for a dinner in a style unique to armed forces chefs and witches around a cauldron.

With HMS *Ocean* being a new ship, she came with a certain number of minor teething troubles that would slowly have to be sorted out at sea. One of these not so minor teething troubles led to a major fire in the AVCAT store. AVCAT is fuel for the turbines, and any fire on a ship is serious enough without the added complication of it involving a fuel storage area. It was also bad timing to find out that the sprinkler system designed to contain such a fire did not work as advertised. At one point, the situation became so serious that an order was made for additional personnel, such as the band, to muster in the hangar deck in preparation to abandon ship! Having been on HMS *Ocean* for a while and taken part in many fire drills and exercises, some of the band assumed that this was yet another of those annoying drills, and presuming so, James Parkinson even went to the hangar wearing only a towel and flip flops. Having got to the muster station and seen that not only was everyone else dressed, they also had their lifejackets with them, James Parkinson quickly returned to clothe his body and acquire a lifejacket.

Tom Scade had a good career in the RMBS before eventually retiring and giving great service to the public in the Scottish Ambulance Service (SAS). Rumour has it that he still has that money he saved in Tortola, and is holding on to it for a rainy day. I can say that, as we are friends and fellow drummers.

Chapter Eight

Yemen: Operation Balsac

Amongst the many and varied duties of the Royal Marines Band Service, one of the most sought after was detached duty on Her Majesty's Royal Yacht *Britannia*. Of course, I am using 'Her Majesty' as at the time HMY *Britannia* was in commission, the late Queen Elizabeth was our much beloved monarch.

On HMY *Britannia*, the band, or 'The golden thirty', as they were known, were usually drawn from the Royal Marines Band Portsmouth. With the band roughly split in two, the Portsmouth Director of Music (DOM) took them aboard, leaving

HMY *Britannia* anchored somewhere exotic for the pleasure Her Majesty, and no doubt, also the RM Band aboard.

behind the bandmaster and the remainder of the band to carry out the daily run of engagements. Not only did you have to be at the top of your musical game to be considered to be selected for service on HMY *Britannia*, you also had to be of a character that would fit in aboard Her Majesty's Yacht without figuratively rocking the boat. There were instances where members of *Britannia*'s crew were quietly returned to their parent unit for minor indiscretions or rule-breaking, so character, leadership and the system of 'old hands' teaching the young members kept the ship squeaky clean in all regards.

One of the many reasons the Royal Yacht duty was so popular was that when accompanying Her Majesty abroad, the locations were usually exotic and the band were well looked after once they had completed their musical duties. Being part of the crew of HM Royal Yacht carried with it a certain status, and within certain parameters, this usually translated into a good run ashore when off duty. Apart from playing for the Royal Family aboard *Britannia*, one of the band's main duties was performing the Beating Retreat ceremony alongside the ship to impress national leaders and local dignitaries. It would be fair to say the band was a firm favourite of the late Queen Elizabeth and she proudly showed them off when HMY *Britannia* visited foreign ports, representing what she and perhaps many would consider the best of British.

At sea, some members of the Royal Family would also on occasion drop into the band mess to chat informally about a programme of music for a dinner, or sometimes, Princess Diana would sit at the piano and ask questions of the pianist about a song she liked. His Majesty The King (formerly known as Prince) was learning the cello, and would ask to sit in or be accompanied while he practised. It was of course a very formal ship, with a very formal rank structure and definition of roles, but music did allow a little blurring of the boundaries, at least in one direction.

Officially, the Royal Yacht *Britannia* always did have a wartime designated role as a hospital ship, but for political and practical reasons was never deployed as such. An example of this was during the Falklands War, when she could possibly have been used for her wartime role, but given the different fuel oil she used compared to the rest of the fleet, that would have added another layer of difficulty to the logistics of the operation. No doubt, there were political considerations about having such a high-profile target in theatre, as there were with the Cunard *Queen Elizabeth 2* liner, also being kept out of harm's way.

Regardless of those constraints, in 1986, while transiting en route to a royal tour of Australia, New Zealand and the Far East, *Britannia* was suddenly ordered to change course and assist with the evacuation of civilians from the beaches of Aden, now called South Yemen. In a part of the world that seems to have endless unrest and turmoil, a civil war had blown up, and uninvolved personnel of many nationalities needed rescuing from the beaches. At short notice, *Britannia* found herself being deliberately sailed into harm's way to assist with an emergency evacuation, under the banner of the very unfortunately titled Operation Balsac.

With the fighting raging ashore and the front line constantly changing, it was down to whichever of the fighting factions had control of the coastal area at that time to allow access and evacuation. Only certain ships were allowed to approach and remove civilians from the war zone, and then only under strict rules, some of which were not adhered to by the combatants. Partly because she could be converted into a hospital ship and because of her non-military appearance, HMY *Britannia* was seen as being acceptable by the fighting factions, and so she, alongside other foreign vessels, began taking evacuees off the beach. Russian vessels also approached to take off their nationals, whilst *Britannia* and the Royal Fleet Auxiliary ship RFA *Bramble Leaf* evacuated British and other foreign nationals who needed to get out.

The evacuation efforts had to be carried out in two stages as some of the small boats available were not suitable to land on the beach, so people were picked up in shallow draught boats, before being transferred to fast speedboats and delivered to *Britannia*. This sensitive operation was undertaken by her crew, the band and some of the Royal Marines Commandos on detached duty to the Royal Yacht. The sailors and Marines' boat-handling skills played an important part in efficiently getting

A hastily shot picture of *Britannia*'s crew transferring refugees from the beach to the ship.

A warm welcome from the band and crew of HMY *Britannia*.

onto and, more importantly, off the beaches when fully loaded with panicking civilians – none of whom wanted to be left behind or, understandably, split up from family members. To help with this and to provide some form of security, some band members were armed and given clear instruction on when they might open fire. Of course, orders and 'rules of engagement' are always given, sometimes quickly and informally, but with the added threat of an international incident involving Her Majesty's Yacht *Britannia*, the armed band members and Marines were given a hard copy of the signal containing their rules of engagement. Band member Mark Oliver still retains his as a memento (or perhaps an aide memoir, should he ever need it again). The content will no doubt be familiar to many.

When read in the cold light of day, rules of engagement can seem to be quite restrictive, which of course they are, but also as if they were written by a lawyer trying to minimise potential litigation, something no one wants to consider while being shot at. Imagine then being a young, talented musician on HMY *Britannia*, embarking on yet another cruise to ports exotic and experiences varied, only to unexpectedly find yourself in a ship's boat, with a gun, heading towards a hostile beach, but luckily for all concerned, carrying a 'Rules of Engagement' order stuffed into your shirt pocket. The personal responsibility and potential wider political consequences of carrying and firing a weapon are huge, but readily accepted by all our armed servicemen and women.

GENERAL RULES

1. IN ALL SITUATIONS YOU ARE TO USE THE MINIMUM FORCE NECESSARY FIREARMS MUST ONLY BE USED AS A LAST RESORT

2. YOUR WEAPON MUST ALWAYS BE MADE SAFE: THAT IS NO LIVE ROUND IS TO BE CARRIED IN THE BREECH AND IN THE CASE OF AUTOMATIC WEAPONS THE WORKING PARTS ARE TO BE FORWARD, UNLESS YOU ARE ORDERED TO CARRY A LIVE ROUND IN THE BREECH OR YOU ARE ABOUT TO FIRE

CHALLENGING

3. A CHALLENGE MUST BE GIVEN BEFORE OPENING FIRE UNLESS TO DO SO WOULD INCREASE THE RISK OF DEATH OR GRAVE INJURY TO YOU OR ANY OTHER PERSON OR YOU OR OTHERS IN THE IMMIDIATE VICINITY ARE BEING SHOT AT

4. YOU ARE TO CHALLENGE BY SHOUTING: QUOTE BRITISH: 'STOP OR I FIRE' UNQUOTE OR WORDS TO THAT EFFECT

OPENING FIRE

5. YOU MAY ONLY OPEN FIRE AGAINST A PERSON:

A. IF HE IS COMMITTING OR ABOUT TO COMMIT AN ACT LIKELY TO ENDANGER LIFE, AND THERE IS NO OTHER WAY TO PREVENT THE DANGER. THE FOLLOWING ARE SOME EXAMPLES OF ACTS WHERE LIFE COULD BE ENDANGERED, DEPENDENT ALWAYS UPON THE CIRCUMSTANCES

[1] FIRING OR ABOUT TO FIRE A WEAPON

B. IF YOU KNOW THAT HE HAS JUST KILLED OR INJURED ANY PERSON BY SUCH MEANS AND HE DOES NOT SURRENDER IF CHALLENGED

6. IF YOU HAVE TO OPEN FIRE YOU SHOULD:

A. FIRE ONLY AIMED SHOTS

B. FIRE NO MORE ROUNDS THAN ARE NECESSARY

C. TAKE ALL REASONABLE PRECAUTIONS NOT TO INJURE ANYONE OTHER THAN YOUR TARGET

The written rules of engagement, to be referred to before opening fire.

The *golden* boys of HMY *Britannia* during Operation Balsac.

Even the royal apartments were pressed into service to accommodate some of the many refugees from the fighting.

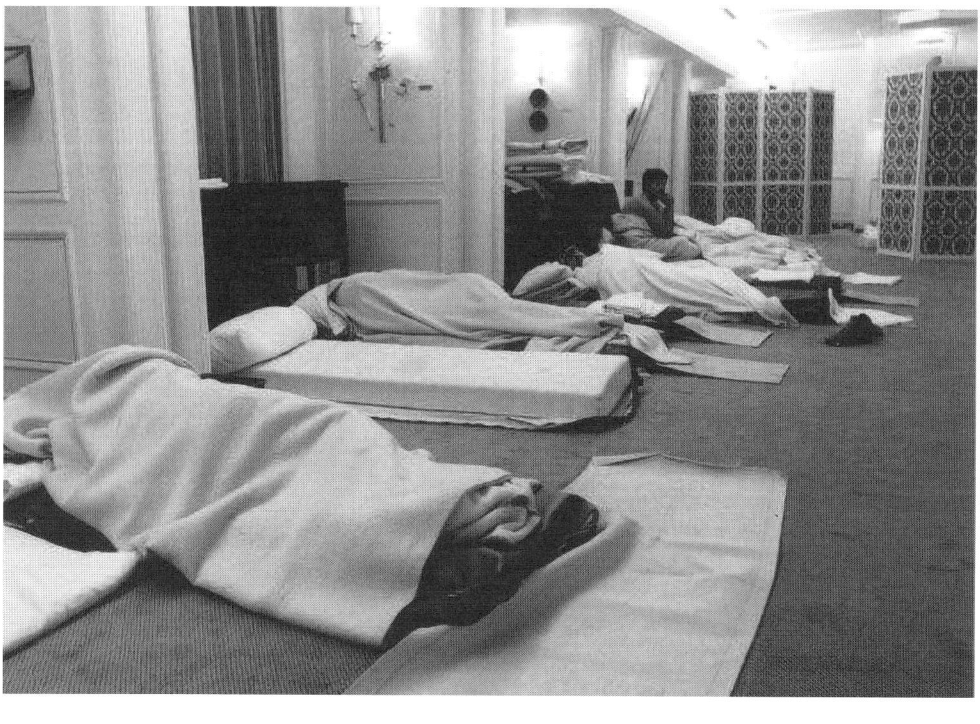

With the evacuation operation in full flow, things were going well until some trigger-happy locals began aiming sniper fire and heavy artillery shelling into the area of the evacuation, forcing HMY *Britannia* to temporarily withdraw to a safe distance. It would take some time and delicate negotiations before another ceasefire could be put in place and she could return to resume the evacuation. Musician Mark Oliver recalls that after completing their boat duties ashore and seeing the dazed evacuees sitting in one of the royal dining rooms, he and some of the band brought out their instruments and played for their newly embarked audience. One rescued female European diplomat was heard to comment: 'Only the British could do this. Amidst gunfire and shelling, here we are drinking tea and listening to a Marines band on the Royal Yacht!'

Mark Oliver's other notable memory from that exciting time in his career is that having given his details to 'Our man in Yemen', the ambassador himself later rang Mark's mother to let her know that her son was safe and was doing a great job. Another role taken on by the band during this operation was gangway security. Former bugler Alan Brooker recalled that some of the people were elderly and all were tired after many days sleeping rough on the beach under gunfire. After much hard and hazardous work, HMY *Britannia* succeeded in rescuing about 450 people of various nationalities, who were taken safely to Djibouti on the African continent.

This operation was not Dunkirk, but along with her officers, crew, RM Commandos and, of course, her band, *HMY Britannia* had given great service in a time of need and proved her worth in a crisis. In current times, when self-praise takes second place to self-criticism, let's leave the final word to that unknown foreign national:

> Only the British could do this. Amidst gunfire and shelling, here we are drinking tea and listening to a Marines band on the Royal Yacht!

Chapter Nine

Wales: The Aberfan Disaster

While researching this book, time and again I found myself not only surprised at the number of non-musical deployments the Royal Marines Band Service has found themselves caught up in, but also the wide range of duties they were asked to perform. This chapter looks at not only one of the most unusual, but also perhaps the most unsavoury and heartbreaking tasks to have been undertaken by musicians.

A chance but timely comment on social media, by former Director of Music John Hillier, set me off researching into RMBS involvement in the Aberfan disaster of 1966. I was surprised and also lucky enough to find musician Brian Roberts, who had vivid memories of his time in the RM Band serving aboard HMS *Tiger*, and importantly to this chapter, of his involvement in the unfolding Aberfan disaster. Early in my research it became clear that depending on your age, the Aberfan disaster is either one of those deeply ingrained national memories, along the lines of Churchill's funeral or the first landing on the moon, or is completely unknown. I hope that this book, as well as having readers of a certain age, will also attract younger readers, so I will start by writing a brief history of how the disaster occurred, before then including the band's contribution to the tragic event.

Mining coal has, or rather had, a long tradition in the Welsh towns and valleys, providing jobs and putting food on the table, and cash into the local economy. The work of digging out coal was both tiring and dangerous, but mostly dangerous to the miners underground in the mile-long caverns, usually not presenting any danger to those outside the mines. As with all mining, in the process of getting to the coal, gold, or desired product, only a small proportion of what is dug out of the ground is actually of any value, so the unwanted residue, known as spoil, is pumped out and stacked high around the mines. As the towns and villages grew up around the same mines the men worked in, they also lived in the shadow of these towering mounds of earth, rock and dust, some of which were well over 100 feet (35 metres) in height and appearing as ugly blemishes on the landscape. The village of Aberfan had seven such spoil tips looking down on it, sometimes casting shadows from a low-setting sun, or blocking out light from a winter sunrise. It was also unfortunate that there was a natural spring running through the hillside where the spoil tips were located, making the ground beneath them inherently unstable

An aerial view of the Aberfan site showing the scale of the destruction.

and no doubt, in hindsight, unsuitable for the purpose. Adding to the spring water from underneath, in mid-October 1966, a period of heavy rain soaked through the spoil tip from the top down, causing it to become even more unstable. Wet through from both above and below, the water turned the slag heap from a solid mass into a semiliquid slurry, which then broke free from its high perch and began its terrible ride into the village below.

Down in the village, life was proceeding as it always had, with the children at the local schools just completing the morning register. The children were quite excited as it was going to be a half day, with the schools closing at 12 o'clock midday to send everyone home for the half-term holiday; but the clocks would soon stop and that time would never come. At 9.15 am, with an ever-increasing roar, a huge torrent of the liquid slurry and rocks rushed down the hillside into the village, hitting houses and completely engulfing Pantglas Junior School. Most of the classrooms were breached and filled to the ceiling with the black all-enveloping semiliquid, taking the lives of all those who were caught in its path. Once the shocked village and mines realised what had happened, the local miners were brought up and rushed to the scene to begin immediate rescue efforts. National resources were also mobilised to try to recover the children and anyone who might have survived the tsunami of dust, dirt and stone, but it soon became clear it was largely going to be an exercise in recovering bodies rather than rescue. The final tally was 116 young children and 24 adults killed, with perhaps the most poignant find being 5 children's bodies huddled around their teacher, as if he was trying to protect them.

My main source for RMBS involvement in this very sad chapter was musician Brian Roberts. Brian joined the Royal Marines Band Service in 1961 and completed his training in 1964, so he had a thorough and comprehensive musical and military education at Deal RM School of Music during his formative years. On completion of his training his first posting was to Eastney, but like so many young musicians (myself included), he was soon sent off to sea to gain not only musical experience but also experience of wider life, usually for the better. Sadly for Brian, one of his early service life experiences was going to be the Aberfan disaster, the effects of which would stay with him and his shipmates for ever.

His ship HMS *Tiger* was a conventional cruiser of the *Tiger* class. Ordered during the Second World War, she arrived too late to see active service and so her peacetime role was as part of the Home Fleet. Bristling with guns, she looked every inch the classic warship, and given her size and ship's complement, warranted a permanent Royal Marines ships size band. She undertook many role changes during her time in service before being retired in 1978 and marked as a reserve ship. As world events in the southern hemisphere unfolded in 1982, she was very nearly brought out of mothballs for the Falklands War, but it was deemed to have been too great an effort in the time required to restore her to full operational capability, and so she did not make it and was eventually sold for disposal. General Thompson, who was a brigadier during the Falklands War and in charge of the invasion, commented that he wished she had been available, as her large guns would have been very useful for naval gunfire support.

The RM Band aboard were a happy group of musicians and the young Brian Roberts felt very much at home on the mess deck amongst his likeminded fellow bandmates. As part of the Home Fleet, HMS *Tiger* had undertaken many long commissions around the globe, but in October 1966, she was in Portsmouth Dockyard preparing to set off on a trip around the British Isles. Brian Roberts, however, had other plans – namely, an important engagement to get married on

HMS *Tiger* at anchor.

15 October, so he was given leave from the ship on the proviso that post-nuptials, he would make his way to Cardiff and rejoin HMS *Tiger* when she arrived there on the 21st. Having got himself married, and presumably having had some sort of short honeymoon, Brian travelled by train and arrived at Cardiff Docks at around 9 am to see his ship come in. Having boarded the ship and rejoined his bandmates, no doubt telling them all about his wedding and accepting their congratulations, rumours started to circulate around the ship that some sort of serious incident had happened ashore at a coal mine and working parties would be needed. The band, along with other crewmembers of HMS *Tiger*, were quickly mustered and given transport up into the Welsh mountains to the Aberfan area, where they were initially told they would be manning road junctions and providing local security, presumably from the press and sightseers. Upon their arrival, it was clear that security was not an issue, but what was needed was manpower at the school to move the tons of earth, rocks and slurry that had enveloped it, in the hope of finding survivors. Once at the school, Brian's heartfelt quote sums it up: 'When we arrived it was the scene

of something out of a horror movie, utter devastation.' He remembers that members of the Salvation Army were some of the first people he saw, and they were giving out free drink and cigarettes to those arriving to help with the rescue, which only added to the surreal situation in which he found himself.

A quick briefing of sorts was given, with an explanation that it was hoped that as the school classroom walls had collapsed domino fashion, there might be spaces and pockets of air where children were trapped and could possibly have survived. The band and other shipmates were put to work, hands on, digging through the outer slurry to reach the school wall itself. By around 3 pm, the rescuers made reasonable progress and reached the inner school, where it was hoped to find survivors. Once the first classroom wall was found, a strong chain was secured underneath and it was lifted up in one piece. What unimaginable horror was ingrained upon the memory of those present when the raised wall revealed the bodies of thirty-two young children, none of whom had had any chance of escape and had died where they lay. Thankfully, it is not something many of us will have to witness, but for the people there that day, it cannot be forgotten, and is forever seared into their individual and collective memories. The hundreds of rescuers continued digging throughout the night, ever hopeful of finding survivors; just one would have made their efforts worthwhile and brought hope. But by the light of day two, it was clear there would be no one coming out alive from that terrible place.

Brian's thoughtful and eloquent words change from graphic details to a more general description, as the memories come flooding back and he decides he has given them more thought than he wants. Reading his words, interpreting the emotion and writing them down have proved emotional even for me as the author, so goodness knows how he has dealt with his thoughts and emotions over the years. I feel bad for having put him through the painful recollection of those days, so I settle for his final comment: 'I could go on if you wish but by the second day it got worse and sometimes some things are best unsaid.' I think Brian did more than his bit back then in 1966, and painfully, once again, for us now to get this story recorded.

In twelve short minutes, with the loss of so many of its young people, Aberfan saw its future change forever. The Welsh mining community gathered from the other hills and valleys to support the village and do what they could, but the pain was visceral and sadness hung in the air. As a show of solidarity and with an attempt to show they could cope, a local dignitary decided a parade would be held through the town of Tonypandy in the Rhondda Valley. Led by the ship's band from HMS *Tiger*, on the following Sunday, the parade took place and was, of course, by its very nature a muted affair but perhaps badly judged given the closeness to the recent disaster. Brian's view was that try as the people might to put on a brave face and show that they could cope, the scale of the disaster was overwhelming and it was clear that many could not.

One of the saddest things about this devastating disaster is that it could have been avoided, if only warnings had been heeded and lessons learnt from previous mining landslips and spoil collapses at this and other mines. Luck, or rather bad luck, also played a part; had it happened a few minutes earlier, the children would not have been in their classrooms, or just a few hours later, the school would have been empty for the half-term holiday.

It feels very strange to be writing a book about music, musicians and the good things they provide in life to then find myself writing about the needless deaths of so many young children. I hope this episode is not as sad for you to read as it was for me to write.

Brian Roberts's career took a more peaceful turn when he eventually left the ship and was sent to the Royal Navy training establishment at HMS Ganges, a shore base in Suffolk. From there, he was moved to the prestigious Staff Band at Deal, a place where there were no musical passengers and you had to be at the top of your game. This should have been a mid-term career stop for Brian, before promotion and other experiences came his way, but in the 1970s, a slashing of defence budgets (sound familiar?) saw redundancies across the services, and Brian was unfortunately one of those nominated to be released back into Civvy Street. He has never been back to Aberfan.

to be used, so antiquated Green Goddess fire engines were brought out of storage and troops and the band trained on them.

The Green Goddess was a relic left over from the post-Second World War National Fire Service (NFS), which even when they were disbanded in 1968, their appliances were deemed out of date and barely fit for service. The vehicle itself was built upon a 1940s-era chassis, with a crash gearbox, which meant the gears would just not sync together when changing gear as in a modern vehicle. No, the driver had to operate the clutch in between gear changes to get the gears to mesh together and avoid a terrible crunching noise. With a travel of around 6 inches (15.5 centimetres), the heavy clutch pedal needed stomping on many times when moving through the gears, the driver's flailing leg looking like he was taking part in a performance of *Riverdance*. The floor of the cab was made of wooden planks (which will become relevant later) and the folding concertina doors could, and did, bite the unsuspecting passenger. I was once caught and trapped in the doors for a short while – the offending marks on my buttocks giving testament to the fierce grip and reluctance of the 'bitey' door mechanism to let me go.

Due to the Goddess being a heavy and unwieldy beast to drive, and as a result of several accidents that occurred as the army was delivering them, it was thought best that some of the band should attend an HGV driving course and have some training with the Royal Corps of Transport (the unofficial yet funny acronym of RCT is deemed not suitable for publication).

I and many other musicians were sent to a desolate army camp near Bovington in Dorset to learn how to drive the vehicles. I say desolate as I cannot recall anything positive about the camp of that time to commend it. Even the supposed oasis of the NAAFI was barren of life as we know it, with the sole crumpled foil Christmas decoration hanging mockingly from the ceiling adding nothing to the festive cheer. The RCT instructors of that time had various ways of encouraging their pupils to correctly initiate a hill start in an army lorry and double clutching. These included (but were not limited to) press-ups and putting your own wristwatch under the back wheel to encourage a good hill start. In little or no time at all (because our watches were now broken), we were all deemed fit enough to drive huge post-war fire engines around the streets of the UK.

On the way to a fire, or 'shout', as they are called, there was a melee in the cab as the band members fought to don their non-waterproof PPE of the day, which essentially amounted to a shiny flasher Mac and Wellington boots. Up front, the driver fought with the vehicle, stomping on pedals and wrestling with the array of gear knobs thoughtfully placed just out of reach for those of average arm length. The large Bakelite steering wheel had a certain amount of play built into it, only effecting the front wheels to turn after a certain amount of waggling back and forth. Not only was the driver fighting with the gears and the notional steering, in the back of the Goddess there was a water tank containing a couple of tons of water (metric tonnes had yet to be invented), which when sloshing around on corners could cause the vehicle to rise up on two wheels, accompanied by the panicked screams of the crew, or on some occasions, causing it to tip over completely, hence the need for driver training.

Emergency calls were usually accompanied by a police vehicle, which led the way with blue lights flashing but seldom getting out of third gear and over 30 miles an hour. Members of the public would stand and watch in awe as vehicles supposedly on their way to an emergency were driving slower than an ice cream van on a council estate.

The Green Goddess was equipped with two small blinking amber lights and a bell, which served little purpose other than to give the crew chief something to do in between screaming at the driver to not kill them. It was because accidents or near misses were happening so frequently that people like me were hurriedly sent on the heavy goods driving course, but having trained in relatively new army lorries that bore little or no relationship to the Green Goddess, some doubted there was any benefit or improvement in driver skills. I am pleased to report that my own driving frightened many but killed nobody, which is perhaps a testament to the instructors of the RCT … or maybe we just got lucky.

Having returned with a shiny new stamp on my licence, I joined the rest of the band from HMS Raleigh at our duty station in HMS Drake, a shore establishment in Plymouth. This suited me as Plymouth was my hometown and I lived close to the barracks. Due to the nature and unreliability of the Green Goddess, usually two were sent together on a shout, giving rise to a certain competition as to who could get there first and deal with the fire.

George Coad was a bugler on my watch and a huge Band Service character of his time; he appears several times in this book. Unimpressed with his bell system and fed up of bugling out of the window, George appeared one day with a set of 'nee-nah' air horns that he had *acquired* (some might say borrowed, others less generously, stolen), and so he spent the early part of the day fitting them to his Green Goddess. After a quick test, George was happy and we – the other crew, who now had horn envy – were not. In the late morning we got our first shout and following the police vehicle we left the barracks with George's Goddess wailing out a strident 'nee-nah', with us following with our feeble bell. Only 100 metres after leaving our base, they suddenly stopped and the crew, coughing, hurriedly exited the vehicle. With George waving us to pass him, his shouted comment 'You go on, we're on fire!' told us everything we needed to know. In his haste to fit the modern air horns to the antiquated Goddess, George had taken some shortcuts and the

Royal Marine Band members found time to keep up their practice with novel ways to announce their arrival at an incident.

overheated wiring had set the wooden cab floor alight. I was hoping to find the pictures of them using their own hoses to put themselves out, but sadly, these are lost to mankind and probably destroyed lest they are used in evidence of George first acquiring the horns and then fitting them without permission.

This may all sound very flippant and fun, and in places it was, but to be fair, there were also many serious fires and incidents that were effectively dealt with by the RMBS. Perhaps the biggest incident was at the Grosvenor Hotel in Glasgow. Many crews were called to attend this huge fire and, in spite of the equipment they were working with, managed to save a good portion of this historic Glasgow landmark. Despite damage totalling £3 million, much to the owners' delight they managed to save the recently renovated terrace portion, which after some remedial work was quickly reopened. Typically, this particular valiant effort does come with another dose of Band Service humour and an intriguing mystery, to boot. When the scale of the fire was realised and further crews requested, members of Stonehouse Band stationed in Glasgow responded. Amongst the chaos of a raging fire, the police and others were surprised to hear them arrive with Bugler Alan 'Bomber' Mills leaning out of the cab playing the cavalry charge. The mystery part of the story occurs post-fire and concerns the whereabouts of many cases of whisky, brandy and gin that were stored in the basement area, which had either evaporated in the overwhelming heat or been removed by *persons unknown* to reduce the fire risk. I think there is a third and much more likely option, but you must make that judgement for yourself.

Of course, the RMBS were not alone manning fire appliances during this time, as there were thousands of soldiers, sailors and marines also deployed, but the addition of intelligent and creative musicians into the mix gave a certain flavour and creativity to the job in hand, along with interesting bugle calls and warning horns fitted to the Green Goddesses. Many of the respondents to my research reported long twelve-hour shifts, sometimes with little happening and sometimes not having enough men or appliances to cover all the required calls, but all seeming to have parts of it to enjoy.

As well as being perched on engines or playing bugle calls not found in any formal music book, some of the enterprising and gigging musicians amongst them played at local pubs in their new locale for free beer. This particular offer to play for drinks instead of cash has caught out many a pub proprietor over the years as the realisation set in that it would have been much cheaper to pay the musicians for their services. However, whatever the cost, it did break down barriers and create a relationship between the locals and those who might save them from a house fire but who could also, at the drop of a helmet, entertain them when off duty.

Regular fire stations and the modern fire appliances in them were out of bounds to the military, although we would sometimes get a cheery wave from picketing firefighters as we slowly rumbled past them in our Green Goddesses (the number of gloved digits they waved being dependent on their current mood). There was a general understanding from them that we, as servicemen, had no choice in being 'strikebreakers', and I think they had some sympathy when they saw the equipment and vehicles we were working with. This chapter might sound like it was all jolly japes, drinking and fun, but it was not. As well as the serious business of being grossly undertrained and underequipped to fight fires, the thousands of servicemen deployed also had to be fed, watered and accommodated, so local barracks, police stations, schools and even sports centres were quickly pressed into service. This led to quite a disparity in the level of comfort and quality of food on offer, depending on where you were based. Some counted themselves lucky to be in schools with the attendant canteens; others experienced military cooking of a kind that would have been banned under the Geneva Convention. If sleeping on a rickety camp bed in the corridor of a junior school was not uncomfortable enough, then trying to wash and shave in the tiny tots' sinks before carefully hovering over the child-sized toilet pan added a new layer of 'fun' to the day.

General Julian Thompson, who has kindly written the foreword to this and my previous book, added an interesting aside to this firefighting chapter. During the firefighters' strike, he was officer in charge of around 1,200 personnel in the Glasgow area, which included members from four different Royal Marines bands. It transpired that most of the musicians had brought their musical instruments, with the exception of one particular band who on orders from their boss had arrived 'unarmed' in the musical sense. Given the good work done when firefighting on duty and the good will produced playing music off duty, the senior officers in charge were annoyed to find one band not functioning as fully it might, resulting in terse messages, signals and phone calls until the matter was put right. A few short years later, General (then Brigadier) Thompson was the officer in charge of the landings to retake The Falklands, and given his long history of working with the RMBS was pleased to have a band attached to 3rd Commando Brigade for the operation.

There is so much more I could have written about the Band Service firefighting in Operation Burberry, but so much of it would have been gratuitous dits, all about their creative and humorous exploits, which could easily give the wrong impression and undermine the excellent work they did as part-time firefighters back in the winter of 1977/8. Buildings were saved, cats were brought down from trees and in some cases, even people's lives were saved by musicians who would rather have been playing music, but having taken the Queen's shilling, exchanged their trombone for a hosepipe and an antiquated Green Goddess that really belonged in a museum.

Chapter Eleven

Firefighting 2: Operation Fresco

Initially I had decided not to write about Operation Fresco, as at first glance I thought it very much mimicked the first firefighters' strike of 1977 and might not add interest, but the more I researched it, the more differences I found. As with that old adage 'The devil is in the detail', this is also true of deployments. So, as they are years apart, involved different personnel, different events and a couple of amusing dits, another firefighting chapter is included. My research also revealed just how many important music engagements were lost, and that is worth noting as the story unfolds. That is my reasoning and I hope you agree, and will enjoy this short chapter, or at least learn something from it.

As before, here's a little bit of background to the deployment. In late autumn 2002, the Fire Brigades Union decided that the time was right for them once again to challenge the government over pay, conditions and cutbacks to the fire service. They had done it before and made some gains and perhaps because now there was a Labour government in power, they felt they could achieve more. I am cleverly, or cowardly, sidestepping the politics and the rights and wrongs of strike action by an emergency service, only to comment that the police do not have such a right to strike. If we lived in a society where they could and did, then, having also worn that uniform and done that job, with all its legal pitfalls, I can only shudder at the thought of the military having to take over the role. Many of my police section were former military and we dealt with incidents in a robust way but backed up by knowing the law and our limits – something that takes a long time to learn and hard-earnt experience to implement.

Also, without the right to strike, once a new firefighters' strike was deemed likely, the military were put on standby. Given the size of the operation and manpower needed to cover a national strike of firefighters, all three services were required to supply and train personnel in the event that the strike went ahead. Against the backdrop of reduced military numbers, standing commitments around the globe and, for those in the know, the premise of another Gulf war just around the corner, finding thousands of additional personnel to cover a strike was a big ask. Each of the services was asked (ordered) to contribute, and so, under the overarching Royal Navy's governance, so too were the Royal Marines and, ultimately, the Band Service. For all the reasons above, the corps was already stretched in other areas, but committed to providing 550 personnel, provided that 200 RMBS musicians could be donated to assist. This was a huge proportion of the Band Service of that time and one can only imagine the resistance, discussion and trump card playing by senior officers to get that to happen, but happen it did.

With RMBS members required almost immediately to begin their firefighting training as drivers, crew and breathing apparatus (BA) wearers, the prospective music programme was slashed, with 75 per cent of the forthcoming musical engagements cancelled. It seems hard to justify such a loss in music terms, but when balanced with having enough boots on the ground to protect life and property, it is easier to rationalise. It would be difficult to justify to someone why they lost a loved one or a house burnt down because somebody needed to hear 'Post Horn Gallop' just one more time! One of the biggest dates in the RMBS calendar is the annual Mountbatten Festival of Music at the Royal Albert Hall. Seen as sacrosanct and one of the highest profile London gigs, the Principal Director of Music (PDM) managed to preserve this event by careful management of what remaining musicians were available, including some of the musicians still under training at the School of Music. As every musician under training already played an instrument on joining, those trainees who were most proficient found themselves playing at the biggest gig of their lives to date, all within a year or two of joining. Along with the many bread-and-butter music gigs that did have to be cut, one of the other major London events had to be rethought. Seen as a showcase for the Royal Marines, the Beating Retreat ceremony on Horse Guards Parade in London was a prestigious showpiece event that had to be downsized dramatically, and performed to a much smaller audience within the grounds of Buckingham Palace. It was not exactly second best in terms of venue, but was a disappointment for the many thousands of members of the public who were not able to attend as normal.

I remember hearing that the Band Service were once more being sent to cover a firefighting strike and thinking that at least since my own participation in 1977, the equipment and vehicles would be better for them this time around: it would be for some, but not for all. It was pot luck on where you were stationed, what was your specific role and what was available for use. It seemed for the majority, the lumbering Green Goddess fire pumps would once again be brought out of mothballs to be a means of transport and source of pumping power at a fire. Already deemed obsolete when retired from the Auxiliary Fire Service in the 1960s, these heavy and unwieldy to drive behemoths were a danger to crew and public alike, especially when fully loaded with water and slurping around a sharp bend. Accidents did happen, as a careless driver or one engaged in the tap-dancing hoedown required to change gear misjudged a corner and universal physics took over. Training did help reduce accidents but not completely. A few lucky units did get an upgrade to

A 1980s-era Dennis fire appliance pressed back into service to take the pressure off the aged Green Goddess.

their engines in the form of 1970s retired Red Dennis or Volvo-style fire engines. Much more modern in appearance and with a synchro gearbox, they were much easier to drive and quicker to get to the fire, but still not as efficient or effective as the modern-day fire engines sitting unused in fire stations. The case was made that to use these engines would inflame (pun intended) the strike situation, and being that the modern engines were much more technical and complicated to operate, the extra training involved would have been lengthy. So it was the old and redundant aforementioned fire appliances that would have to be used.

The two main respondents who helped with this chapter are both former percussionist students of mine from the Royal Marines School of Music who, despite my teachings and perceived wisdom, both went on to have successful careers in the RMBS.

Chris Chalkley was based in HMS Flying Fox in Bristol, a shore establishment for reservists, where he was a crew commander of a fire appliance. In charge of a mixed crew from different services, he spent a lot of his time keeping his young army driver under control. This was not in a bad way, just that the young driver was very keen, and at the first ring of the telephone would run to the fire engine and start revving the engine, only to be pulled out and told it was the call that lunch was ready. There is a thin line between keenness and enthusiasm, and a thinner line between patience and annoyance – a line that his driver crossed on a daily basis.

Chris Chalkley remembers that many of the fires they attended were rather ordinary, except for one where a local character, well known to the police, had once again had his car torched for some extra-marital transgression. The other reason it was notable was that it was one of the only occasions the police did not have to fight with him, so maybe percussionist's charm does exist?

Chris's main claim to fame during the strike was that out of the many thousands of servicemen involved in Operation Fresco, Sky News chose him to take part in a TV interview. In true percussionist style, he, with his confidence far exceeding his actual knowledge of the subject matter, blagged his way through a live interview on national television. It appears my tutelage had not been completely in vain.

As in the 1977 strike, there was very little animosity from the striking firefighters directed at the military. Intelligent and with many of them ex-forces themselves, there appeared to be an understanding that the military had no choice but to deploy and with their limited equipment and experience, could only just about stay on top of it, thereby perhaps easing the firefighters' social conscience. Chris and his crew would often be stopped by the striking firefighters as they passed by the fire station, ostensibly for a goodwill chat and to be offered food, but invariably, when they returned to HMS Flying Fox, it would be found that the rear of the Green Goddess would be covered in firefighters' strike stickers. It was done in good spirit and with a sense of humour borne of a shared experience, and worth it for the free food they were given.

Here is another of those 'it's not about me but' warnings. When I was in my second career as a police officer in Dover, me and a colleague were sent to a cold and wet Dover Docks to keep an eye on animal rights protesters. Deciding to engage politely with them through the police car window to avoid getting wet seemed at the time a good compromise. That was until at the end of a long shift, and many blue light calls around Dover, we returned to the police station and found we had spent the entire shift covered in animal rights stickers. They no doubt delighted that we had spent our shift inadvertently promoting their cause.

Dave Prentice was my other main source for this chapter – the very same Dave Prentice from the African Ebola operation in an earlier chapter. At the time of the deployment, Dave was in the band at Dartmouth (BRNC), who were some of the first musicians put on notice to deploy. As such, they had the benefit of several weeks' training at the Royal Naval Air Station (RNAS) at Culdrose, in Cornwall. With RNAS Culdrose being an airfield, it also had a good firefighting training facility and highly experienced navy firefighters to conduct the training. Dave and his crew were earmarked as a breathing apparatus and rescue team (BART), which

Former percussionist and now a paramedic, Dave Prentice is dressed in his breathing apparatus for the Operation Fresco duties.

on paper and in practice is one of the more dangerous roles, as you can be reasonably (or unreasonably) expected to enter burning buildings with your breathing apparatus set on to rescue people.

Post-training, Dave and his crew were sent to operate from a Territorial Army (TA) base in Ellesmere Port near Liverpool, working alongside the Royal Horse Artillery (RHA), who were also on firefighting duty but this time without their horses. The BART team had a specialised vehicle for their role, which was a flatbed truck to hold their breathing apparatus and Clansman cutting equipment. Their vehicle was appreciatively quicker than the RHA horsemen of the apocalypse in their Green Goddesses, their progress made even quicker by having police outriders as escorts leading them to the incidents and clearing the way for them through traffic lights. Dave and his crew attended many incidents, but nothing was quite as intense as the training at RNAS Culdrose, Ellesmere Port and Manchester Airport. At all three of the sites they had been subjected to entering huge purpose-built firehouses containing flames and smoke, before crawling on hands and knees in breathing apparatus to find a heavy dummy casualty that they had to drag from the burning building. Such was the length and quality of the firefighting training that none of the actual fires and incidents they attended came anywhere close to what they had experienced, and so were dealt with quickly and competently. The old expression 'Train hard, fight easy' could apply.

In the introduction to this chapter, I explained the reasons for including a second, short firefighting chapter, which I hope you have found a worthwhile read. The people, equipment and incidents were different and I think for their work alone it was worth recording. I am wary of including similar stories just for the sake of filling pages – something none of us needs – so apart from a passing well done to the RMBS for the Operation Fresco service of 2002, this chapter is now at a close.

together. Assuming then that in the case of orthodox Russian military aggression, an invasion could be held back by the forces ranged against them, and the conflict had not yet escalated into nuclear war, then the local threat to the UK mainland would need to be addressed. In the absence of wholescale invasion by a foreign adversary and assuming that the United Kingdom had not become a nuclear wasteland, a third, more sinister, threat was perceived, that being the insertion of spies or paramilitary teams of Russian Spetsnaz (special forces). These teams would be expected to attack key points of the country's infrastructure, military bases and airfields; commit assassinations; and generally undermine the workings of the government. Hence, Exercise Brave Defender was put into operation to test the local home defences against any such attacks. A military planner somewhere decided the best defence against Russian Spetsnaz would include Royal Marines musicians, and whilst I am sure there are times when a badly scratched violin or raucous bass trombone might deter an assailant, I am equally sure that special forces are made of tougher stuff, or at least are issued with earplugs. Regardless, a box was ticked and we were summoned to participate in the exercise – or, perhaps, ordered would be a more accurate description.

As well as military and medical training for Royal Marines musicians of that era, during the 1980s many of the bands were also given the role of defending key points, or KPs, as they were known. During those bands' annual military training weeks, the emphasis shifted away from first aid and casualty evacuation to the finer points of guarding a KP. Whilst most military training was regarded by the musicians as a trial and time away from music, guarding the KPs added a new level of tedium hitherto unknown, boredom both during lectures and when actually carrying out the role. It is hard to enthuse the active musician's brain with hours of guarding and displaced sleep when there is no active threat other than the training teams, the local enemy within.

I know this will gain little, none or even negative sympathy from soldier types, but that's just how it works: we musicians joined to play music, not to play soldiers, and your love of camouflage cream and gritty eyes does not easily cross the border into our world. Those bands in the 1980s, like the one based in HMS Raleigh in Cornwall, spent the majority of their annual military training weeks guarding old forts and barracks in the local area. Tregantle Fort in south-east Cornwall was a favourite for these exercises, with the cold, stone Napoleonic fort providing none of the comforts of home such as windows or lighting, leaving the dark and windy emplacements the last place you would want to stand a four-hour guard duty. This might sound like a musician whining (which it is) but it is leading to a point. The enemy trying to 'get in' at night to attack the pretend KP or, in this case fort, were usually members of the same training team who were instructing us during the day. So, being Royal Marines Commandos, not only did they have the military edge over the band but they also knew how, where and when to gain entry, so invariably we lost and they won. This is relevant because a similar system was also in place when attending military promotion courses, when the training team were once again playing the part of both instructor and enemy, so they always had the advantage. The important difference between those circumstances and Exercise Brave Defender was that the training teams were now deployed with us and had a reputational stake in defending against whoever was playing the enemy, which, in most cases, was the UK's top special forces from the SAS and SBS.

Despite many of the Band Service desperately looking for reasons to avoid Exercise Brave Defender, including one creative individual who booked a vasectomy for that week, unless you had a cast-iron excuse, were deemed absolutely essential at your home base, or had a medical reason for not using condoms, then you were going on the exercise, like it or not.

The band I was in was told to report to the Commando Training Centre at Lympstone (CTCRM) to draw equipment and weapons. Resplendent in what was obviously newly issued camouflage suits and wearing our green berets in various nonchalant ways and at jaunty angles, the band paraded with the training teams for a briefing from senior Commando officers. Being a West Country based band, we assumed we would once again be walking the ramparts of an ancient fort, somewhere local, where perhaps the pasty is the main meal of the day, but assumption in the military is a dangerous and hopeless enterprise, which brings the beholder down at the first fence.

The briefing by the officers gave us our first idea of the huge scale of the exercise we were taking part in, and also where the KP that we would be guarding was situated. For reasons best known to military planners, or at least the dice they were using, we were to board coaches and head many hundreds of miles up the length of the UK to Northumbria, which, for those of you like me who are geographically challenged, it is near where England meets Scotland, and not in a good way. Our destination and KP was a disused RAF missile site, which consisted of a ring of deadly looking 1960s-era Bloodhound missiles arranged in a circle. Given the open area around the missiles and huge expanse of Forestry Commission woodland beyond, to the untrained eye it would seem not too difficult a target to protect from any special forces sent against us, be they Russian Spetsnaz or those home-grown sneaky chaps from Hereford or Poole, where the SAS and SB are based.

The band was split into sections and into these were added junior Marine Commandos under training, and as such wore their blue berets. Some of these junior Marines had difficulty adjusting from the ways of their Commando corporal trainers to the softer tones and attitudes of us band corporals. However, as the

An RAF Bloodhound missile site from the 1960s.

exercise progressed this would change and adjustments to attitudes had to be made both ways. With some of the Commando training team sergeants running our HQ, communications and organising the sections, we now genuinely felt we were part of the same team, and the 'them and us' feeling that pervaded other training courses was now gone. All that remained was for us to defeat the enemy and save the missiles from the foe, and we could all go back to the status quo.

For several days, band corporals, musicians and junior Marines patrolled about the Northumbrian landscape seeking out the enemy, while the hungry midges sought us out. At night we stumbled around dark, infested forests, or propped ourselves in carefully planned observation points (OPs) to watch the enemy's likely approach routes. With no obvious attacks in evidence (other than the gnats) and with the last night of the exercise upon us, an all-out effort was made to protect our KP and maintain the 100 per cent reputations of our sections and training team.

My section was left for most of the night lying in a damp forest watching access from a road, when, in the early hours, some quiet but distinct noises could be heard and were reported by radio to the training team. Quiet, sneaky beaky footsteps were so close I could not risk speaking into the radio, and so had to communicate with HQ by just pressing the transmit button to answer questions from the now tense training team by clicking once for yes, two for no. Refused permission to open fire (with blanks) as we could not positively identify the targets, and with an attack on the KP evidently imminent, we were told to up stumps and return to the main missile base. Having returned to a warm welcome, something unheard of from training teams, still in darkness, my section was placed on the perimeter as we formed part of a giant circle around the missile launchers. The tension was palpable as around us other musicians and Marines watched the clock tick down towards Endex and our success. As the early dawn started to break and we could see the other sections strategically placed around the missiles, it seemed that just for once we were going to win. Happy with our efforts, smug looks and nods of approval were handed out to one and all as the sun broke through the early misty morning. Then, there was a huge bang behind us and smoke emanated from the missile positions we had been guarding. There was an overwhelming feeling of disappointment that somehow, through all the long nights, gnat bites, patrols and keen guarding, we had failed. This was only slightly offset by the high regard for the skill of our unseen special forces, who had against all the odds managed to carry out their attack. Some of us did think perhaps the explosive device had been planted well before the start of the exercise and therefore we were always going to lose, but that would have been cheating, would it not?

It was a long drive back to CTCRM in a convoy of coaches, but even tired faces recognised equally tired faces of other troops in coaches going the other way. At CTCRM, kit was returned and faces were washed, and one or two of the band corporals got a 'well done' from some of the training team and officers involved. One of the band corporals even got a recommend for giving a bollocking to a wayward South African junior Marine who had some issues and needed an attitude adjustment. Not only was the bollocking a good one, the corporal had gone to the trouble of learning a couple of Afrikaans swear words to ram home his point: *Dit word baie as baie goed gesien!*

Portsmouth band also had a similar experience but their KP was at a former United States Air Force Base at Bruntingthorpe in Northamptonshire. Having heard from some of the band, not only did they claim that they had defeated their enemy, but that the fight was so epic it became to be known as the Battle of Bruntingthorpe! Given there are no independent witnesses to the said 'battle', and as far as I am aware no plaque or memorial has been erected, then any such questions about it should be directed to members of the Royal Yacht Band directly.

Former Bugler Mark Snell was in the band at Deal, and being *the* staff band with the Principal Director of Music at the helm, they felt sure they would be left to cover the musical diaries of other bands while Brave Defender took place. Fate, and the hand of a senior officer, intervened and Deal Staff Band found themselves hundreds of miles away, perched on a Welsh hilltop. Having accepted the challenge, this was now their KP to guard and their training team and Royal Marines major in charge were not going to give it up without a fight. On one bleak night guarding the KP, noises were heard, and as some of the band prepared to investigate, they were stopped by their Commando-trained officer. In hushed tones, he explained that the enemy were probably trying to find where the sentries were positioned, provoke a response and thereby identify guard posts. Nodding sagely at this new military wisdom, they all huddled down and remained quiet so as to not reveal their positions. The major decided the time was right to sneak a peek over the wall but his timing was out (or the enemy's timing was in) as a fist-sized lump of Welsh granite hit him squarely on the head and knocked him backwards into the huddle of Bandies. Such was the injury that the officer had to be real-world casevaced out of the exercise and did not return.

Another Deal-based musician who found himself guarding this particular key point in the Welsh Mountains was Paul Slator. A fine trombone player, guitarist and with a keen sense of humour, Paul's neutral wry smile often concealed (and still does) what he was actually thinking. I know this as I still direct Paul and others in the annual Deal charity pantomime. In this year's show (*Peter's Pans*, 2024), I cast him as a 2-year-old wearing a babygrow, which he accepted without even a raised eyebrow – just a knowing look and that wry smile. I hope that with me having explained something of Paul's character and intellect you can see how the prospect of many hours and days of boring guard duty would not have appealed to him. So, to alleviate the boredom, Paul fashioned a chess set out of rocks and anything else that looked like it could be a chess set. In truth, this small dit might not have made the chapter had he not provided a picture as evidence of his endeavours and creative DIY skills.

Being part of Brave Defender was definitely outside the Band Service members' normal comfort zone and certainly could not be described as enjoyable, but it was interesting to be part of a national exercise. It also came with the added bonus of seeing a member of a Royal Marines Commando Training team smile, albeit through gritted teeth.

After Endex, the experience and skills learned though Brave Defender were not completely lost to the band when, a year later, they undertook their normal annual military training. This time they were ordered to guard an old Second World War airfield at Dunkeswell in Devon, but back to the old cat-and-mouse routine with their training team again playing the enemy. The musicians learnt (as musicians do) that when the lights went on in the toilet of the defunct control tower, the training team were now awake and getting ready to attack or cause havoc. When at 4 am the lights were reported to a certain band sergeant, the opportunity for some payback, and to show that bandy could do it, proved irresistible. To stop

Musician Paul Slator found a creative way to pass the long hours guarding the KP by making a chess set from things he found in the natural environment.

a potential vehicle-borne improvised explosive device (IED) attack on the main gates, the band sergeant ordered an ambush to be set up on the approach road with all the firepower at his disposal. Some will say his briefing was reminiscent of Russell Crowe in the film *Gladiator*, with the words 'At my signal, unleash hell!' Others have a less dramatic recollection. In spite of us only having blank rounds, two general-purpose machine guns (GPMG), self-loading rifles (SLR) and flares, they were all held in eager trepidation for the attack. At what seemed about the expected time, vehicle headlights were seen driving along the airfield perimeter track; they then turned directly towards the KP and the hidden musicians lying in wait. Imparting his best Russel Crowe impression, 'NOW!' shouted the sergeant, and all hell of blank firing and chaos broke loose, the noise and sparks creating a visual and audio spectacle, added to by the firing of parachute flares towards the car as pretend missiles. The car violently swerved, narrowly missing some trees and a ditch before coming to a halt. Having given the command to 'cease fire', under the now relative silence, screams could be heard emanating from the vehicle. Still in military mode and not wanting to be caught out by any training team tricks, the band sergeant and protection team approached the vehicle in a cautious and weapons pointed manner. The door was opened by a near-hysterical and pale-faced

seize control of the Suez Canal, but due to lack of international political support from certain quarters it was ultimately unsuccessful, with many losses, including thirteen Royal Marines killed. The story of that and many more operations can be found in Dr David Abrutat's excellent and comprehensive book *Four Two: The Official History of 42 Commando, Royal Marines 1943–2023*, published by the Royal Marines Historical Society.

Back at Exercise Bright Star, set amongst the vast international backdrop of cooperation, in 1999 it seemed that some of the 85,000 participants required to make the exercise a success were the Band of HM Royal Marines, Commando Training Centre, and also the Band of Britannia Royal Naval College. CTCRM band were flown out first to Naples in Italy, where they joined HMS *Ocean*. Looking very much like a traditional aircraft carrier, HMS *Ocean* was officially designated as a landing platform helicopter (LPH), and although based on the *Invincible*-class aircraft carrier hull, her superstructure and flight deck were designed and built for helicopters, and her interior as an amphibious assault ship. Only commissioned in 1998, she was still smart and shiny for Exercise Bright Star, and an ideal vessel for the task. With the band on board and the exercise underway, one of their first duties was unusual and less than military. For reasons best known to the organising officer, an officers' formal dinner was arranged in the middle of the desert. This of course would need the traditional tune 'The Roast Beef of Old England' to be played by the band as the guests assembled, and presumably, 'The Goat of Old Cairo' to be played as the main course was paraded around the tables and served. No doubt, the unique setting was the main reason for the unusual dinner venue and the band played their part in creating a suitable atmosphere.

The other RM band in theatre was the band of Britannia Royal Naval College (BRNC), which having been plucked from the beautiful retiring backwater of Dartmouth, now found itself in Egypt. Acting in their medical role, they were attached to the Medical Squadron as part of the Commando Logistics Regiment. Commando Logistics, and in fact all logistics, are obviously a very big part of warfare, as ably demonstrated by the logistics chain that supported the United Kingdom's recovery of the Falkland Islands some years earlier. Faced now with some similar and yet some vastly different challenges, the Medical Squadron was well supported by its logistics supply chain. With some pre-planning and on-site training, by the time the exercise started it had already integrated the band members into its infrastructure, and they were assured they could do the jobs required of them. The Medical Squad's plan required BRNC band personnel to split into two sections and deploy, and to operate two separate Forward Dressing Stations (FDS). As the name implies, these are, in effect, first aid posts where casualties can receive second-line care, one step from the battlefield, where they will have been initially and urgently treated by comrades and medics in the field before being passed back along the medical evacuation chain.

If required, it is also where any nuclear fallout, biological or chemical agents used (if actually used or simulated) would be removed and the person decontaminated. I will be happy to be advised on postmillennial methods, but in the 1970s, 80s and 90s, the main hands-on method was the liberal application of an inert talcum powder-like substance called Fuller's earth. This very fine powder would (at least, that is what the training promised) absorb and remove all the known nuclear, biological and chemical agents of its time, provided, of course, it was applied repeating the 'Bang, blot, rub' mantra. However effective this might have been in practice, in exercise it merely provided minutes of entertainment squirting the powder into an unsuspecting casualty's respirator (gas mask).

With BRNC operating the forward dressing stations, some were very surprised to see some of the exercise's pretend casualties to be fellow RM musicians from CTCRM. Being such a relatively small branch of the Royal Marines, and coming from another West Country based band just up the road from each other, friendships were rekindled, stories shared and, no doubt, one or two respirators filled for good measure.

The testing of Medical Squadron to adequately support the 3rd Commando Brigade was a great success, as was their ability to quickly adapt, and move the forward dressing stations at short notice to meet the demands of the RM units and the exercise. Quickly leapfrogging by road and air gave medical cover when and where it was needed, for which the RMBS personnel were given credit for their flexibility. CTCRM band also brought credit upon themselves when in the field as well as when taking up their instruments amidst the medical duties of the exercise. When back on HMS *Ocean*, the band even put their training into a real-life scenario when a damaged Chinook helicopter had to make an emergency landing on the ship and they were required to be on duty as medics. Once the exercise was officially over (Endex), there was then time for more music to be played and some well-earned downtime for all. During an event known as 'Distinguished Visitors' Day', the then Secretary for Defence inspected the band and made a point of telling them that 'everyone was talking about the band's performance over the last few weeks' – high praise indeed from the lofty heights of government.

Chapter Fifteen

Exercise Northern Merger

The last of our musical excursions into the land of military exercise takes us back to 1974, to an event called Exercise Northern Merger. Although it sounds like the financial amalgamation of two Yorkshire building societies, it was actually a rather serious Royal Navy and Royal Air Force joint exercise, with an amphibious landing by Royal Dutch Marines thrown in for good measure. It included major Royal Navy ships of the day such as the aircraft carriers HMS *Hermes* and HMS *Bulwark*. The *Bulwark*, which still had the appearance of an aircraft carrier, had been converted in 1958 for use and designated as a Commando carrier for amphibious assault operations. In an exercise of close cooperation with fellow marines, on board were our close military counterparts, the Dutch Marines.

Working with the Dutch Marines, or 'Cloggies', as they are colloquially known, is not an unusual occurrence, with our Royal Marine Commandos frequently cross-training with them and taking part in exchange postings to gain wider knowledge of each other's military skills and equipment. The Dutch are also an important part of NATO, and so any chance to train, exercise and integrate together was and still is welcomed. With their own unique language forming a formidable communication barrier, luckily, like many of our European neighbours, most of the Dutch speak good English, so military communication, socialising and humour are generally not a problem. Indeed, there are some that say the Dutch people speak better English than a Scouser talking football to a Geordie.

Having been invited to partake in Exercise Northern Merger, which was based in Scotland and the North Sea, the Dutch could have reasonably expected the part of the opposing enemy to have been played by the Scottish-based 45 Commando Royal Marines, but due to their own operational requirements, 45 Commando were deployed elsewhere. With 45 Commando being 'out of town on business', their Scottish base, called RM Condor, was relatively empty, with just some headquarters personnel and a small training team left behind. This team was going to put the Royal Marines Band of Flag Officer Scotland & Northern Ireland through their annual military training. This ten-day military training period was not exactly looked forward to by FOSNI band, as like musicians everywhere, they preferred the feel of an instrument in their hands to an oily weapon, and the embrace of a cold beer glass to the hot metal mess tins that a coffee of sorts was served in. That aside, anyone without a valid excused chit was present, even if incorrect, and the training got underway.

Corporal Bugler Chris 'Dan' Archer, who would later become Drum Major Archer, provided me with a wealth of information about this exercise, most of which has been redacted to protect the innocent, the guilty and the reputation of the Dutch Marines. As in the aircraft carrier chapter, Chris Archer is well known throughout the Band Service as 'Dan', and therefore referred to as such here.

With introductions made, the band were relieved to find that despite being a dyed-in-the-wool platoon weapons instructor, their main RM Commando instructor was 'band friendly', and from experience already knew their skill set, their mindset and perhaps most importantly, their sense of humour. The training began with some back-to-basics weapons refresher training, followed by first aid and map reading, but then, unusually, some small section attack and ambush drills – something that was normally outside of the band's military training syllabus. Section drills in the military are the bread and butter for infantry soldiers and amphibious troops, but less so for musicians. Interestingly enough, though, for active minds, the band and bugle corporals all readily accepted the challenge of leading sections attacks and suitably impressed the PWI and his training team with their enthusiasm.

After a few days of learning what Royal Marines Commandos take several years to perfect, the band were boarded onto Land Rovers and sent out in their various sections to patrol an area near a beach, and there to set up their own secure base camp. This would require communications to be set up and the band sleeping in 'bivvies' for a couple of nights. Bivvy is short for bivouac, which can apply to any temporary cover, shelter or rough accommodation when sleeping out in wartime, on exercise, or if you are in the Scouts. In this case, it meant using simple plastic ponchos to make tent-like covers and prepare basic places to sleep. With everything seemingly going well, the band at this point thought there would be a few nights under the stars, before hearing their own Endex, which is the most welcome signal or order given that a tired body in the field can hear. The hot bath, the cold beer and the smell of real coffee could be anticipated and almost tasted as the days and hours ticked down to Endex.

With some sections sent out on patrols, Dan Archer's was sent to a beach and told to set up an observation point amongst the sand dunes and report any movements or suspicious activity. Having deployed his section, Dan patrolled to the edge of the sand dunes to investigate suspicious noises and was amazed to see he was in front row seats for a full-scale amphibious landing by the Dutch Marines. The assault, complete with helicopters, landing craft and Buccaneer aircraft flying support, was in full swing when one of the Buccaneers flew so low over Dan's section that they could see the pilot, and he could see them. Dan and his section pulled back and returned to their patrol base to brief their training team platoon weapons instructor. It was at this point the PWI shared the news that yes, there was an exercise, and yes, they were now in it, playing the part of an opposing enemy force. Anyone who has ever played the part of *the enemy* knows it is all about harassing and putting pressure on the troops in the exercise, whilst also having some fun in the process. The basic premise is that the rules of engagement for opening fire and of general fairness only apply to the exercise troops, and the enemy can generally do as they please. The band members now realised why they had been issued so much blank ammunition for their rifles and general-purpose machine guns and also things like hand-held parachute flares called Schermulys to light up the night sky.

I do have to take you on a little detour at this point as the mention of the Schermuly brings back my own military training, where the flares were used as hand-launched rockets at 'enemies and cars' during the hard-fought but easily lost Battle of Dunkeswell in 1983. (This was not a real battle but actually another exercise.) More pertinent is that there is a military drill to be followed if you are caught out in the open when someone pops a parachute flare. The drill initially involves going to ground if you see or hear the rocket going up, but if you are caught when it opens, then you instantly freeze. With the flare wobbling under the parachute as it slowly descends, troops were told to also slowly wobble to the ground to mimic the movement of the light and shadows cast. It might sound ridiculous (because it is) but to soldiers it was a serious drill that had to be played out. If, however, it was not in a real war situation, then it was hilarious to watch sections of troops self-consciously wobbling to the floor like deflated blow-up dolls.

Back at their patrol base camp, with the band and the PWI now all on the same team, the band corporal section commanders took their instructions and gave their own set of orders. The NATO sequence of orders is a standard format that ensures all the pertinent information for the mission is given to the troops under your command. The basic headings are Situation, Mission, Execution, Administration and Logistics, and Command and Signal. Each of these headings has subsections and quite often the briefings will be accompanied by a map or rough handmade model of the terrain.

The band's orders in short were to oppose the enemy landings and harass them as they came further inshore. Some thirty-plus years later, in his reply to my research, I think you can still sense the joy in Dan Archer's excited comment: 'You can imagine the band's attitude. We had gone from a training week to now being a guerrilla force with wads of ammo, thunder flashes and smoke grenades, with our orders being to hassle the Dutch Marines!'

Now the proverbial gloves were off, the band apparently took to this task with relish, with even some of the old and bold musicians who did not love their GPMG as much as they should being prepared to clean it post-firing, if needed. In a very military and tactical way, Dan Archer's section set out at night, following various compass headings to locate the Dutch headquarters. With night navigation not being their forte, I think it came as something of a surprise to everyone (including themselves) that they found they were somewhere near to the enemy HQ, near enough to attract the attention of some alert Dutch sentries. Undeterred, the section set up their GPMG in a flanking position and having carried the heavy weapon throughout the night, were now determined to fire it. This section were amazed to see that their flanking manoeuvre had caught the Dutch sentries by surprise and watched as they now beat a hasty retreat, no doubt to report they had made contact with the enemy.

Other band sections had also been patrolling and looking for the Dutch Marines, and perhaps given their limited night map-reading skills, more by luck than judgement had now found them. Two of the sections now had the Dutch HQ in their sights from slightly different directions and about 500 meters apart. Dan Archer heard some Dutch Marines speaking Dutch, moving up the beach towards him, and so hastily set up an ambush with a three-badge trombone player on the GPMG and himself on the flank with a self-loading rifle. 'Three badge' refers to someone who has served a long length of service in the Marines/navy, but never considered offering themselves up for promotion, so essentially still a musician or bugler with a rank equivalent to a private.

From his vantage point Dan witnessed the other band section suddenly break cover and attack the Dutch headquarters from behind. The Dutch HQ staff, who were stood outside casually smoking, had been caught completely by surprise by the 'Bansai Bandies' charging into their camp. The attack was finished by much shooting and the throwing of Thunderflashes and smoke grenades into the Dutch command post, rendering it captured and ruined by the smoke. With the enemy HQ overwhelmed, Dan Archer and his trombone gunner were not to be outdone and so opened fire (with blanks) on another group of Dutch Marines who had run into his ambush and killing ground. The cacophony, spectacle and surprise result was enough for the exercise umpire, who blew his whistle to end the battle. The umpire, being a Royal Marines major, was suitably impressed with the section attacks and congratulated the Royal Marines on their ambush drills. However, his jaw dropped somewhat when he asked if they were from 45 Commando, only to be told they were FOSNI band on their annual military training. Roaring with laughter, the major tried to explain to the Dutch Marines they had been bumped not by RM Commandos, but RM musicians. As if it needed further validation, the appearance of the GPMG trombone gunner, wearing his ankle puttees wound up his leg like a Japanese sniper, helped put things into perspective, but not a perspective the Dutch enjoyed.

The battle on the beach was won but the exercise war was scheduled to continue until the following morning. Following their orders to harass the Dutch, the band sections once again attacked at first light, just as the Dutch were packing up and preparing to re-embark their landing craft. The signal to open fire was the firing of a Schermuly, which did have the desired signalling effect, but in the firing came close to hitting a Royal Navy Wessex helicopter swooping low over the beach. Shooting down one of the Royal Navy's helicopters is never deemed acceptable, but luckily for all concerned, it narrowly missed the chopper. Only the crewman's shocked face as he stood in the open door recorded just how close it had come.

At the official Endex, the band unofficially called the score FOSNI band 2: Dutch Marines 0, but that is not to take anything away from the Cloggies' military skill set; perhaps they were a bit unlucky. Just what the incredulous and perhaps embarrassed Dutch officers thought about being bounced by FOSNI band is not recorded anywhere, at least not in English. It was probably best forgotten by them and never again spoken about when they got home. But from time to time, a very proud Royal Marines Commando PWI instructor tells the story at mess dinners of 'that time the band stopped an invasion'!

Chapter Sixteen

Northern Ireland: Operation Banner

At this point in the book, we turn away from the softer deployments, civilian assistance and military exercises, towards the harder and more military deployments that contained real-world dangers that ordinary musicians are not usually expected to face.

This chapter about Northern Ireland might come as surprise to most, including many of the wider Royal Marines Corps itself. I expect that none of our Commando brethren will recall having seen bandy when they were slogging through bandit country in South Armagh in the rain, or climbing down from a border watchtower after a long and miserable shift, because for all the obvious reasons, bandy was not there. However, there will be a small group of Marines with unfavourable memories of bandy being there, and of being roused from much needed sleep by listening to them ... but more of that later. The RMBS deployments to the Northern Ireland province certainly were regular but much shorter, and they were sent there for a much different role to our military troops – perhaps, surprisingly or not, to play music. As to why musicians would be sent to such a trouble spot, sometimes covertly armed, sometimes overtly musical, will be set out below, but they were not sent there to patrol or take part in the policing of the troubles.

There cannot be many people who are unaware of the Northern Ireland troubles and the ensuing terrorist violence that it produced. The complicated history of the province, added to by religious and sectarian divides, provided for many decades of terrorism and violence, arguably peaking in the 1970s and 80s. Thrown into the mix to help quell the violence, all facets of the British military were involved in assisting the local police authorities. As well as trying to suppress the violence from both sides by patrolling and proactively gathering intelligence, other covert assets were in place to try to undermine the terrorists' efforts, but not always successfully. It was a time when the security forces could be sniped at, ambushed, or blown up by a bomb, as the Royal Marines Commandos of that era knew only too well, as they undertook many operational tours there.

Into this cauldron of political strife and terrorist violence, someone, somewhere, decided it would be a good idea to add military musicians, and so over a period of about ten years, RM bands from both Scotland and Plymouth made regular visits to Northern Ireland to play music in a variety of surreal situations. Now this might not sound like a deployment of the kind ascribed to in the rest of this book, but for the musicians involved the trips were stressful and worrying, which I expect will draw little (if any) sympathy from military ranks posted there for many months at a time.

Before you could play any music, of course, you had to get there, and how you actually travelled to Northern Ireland was dependent on which of the bands you were serving in. Plymouth band were in the habit of flying into Belfast on commercial flights from Bristol or Exeter airports, whilst Scotland band used the civilian ferry to cross the Irish Sea. Because of the volatile and tense situation at that time, Scotland band made the journey unaccompanied, in civilian clothes, and with the senior non-commissioned officers (NCOs) and their director of music (DOM) covertly armed with concealed pistols. This unusual arrangement led to some interesting occurrences, as concealed weapons in tight-fitting suits were perhaps not always as concealed as they might have been, and, on occasion, obvious to civilian onlookers. There are many dits surrounding those armed sea crossings, many of which have passed into Band Service folklore. Having tracked down those who were there, I have accepted their veto of these stories and am not repeating them here – partly for security reasons and partly to spare any embarrassment of those good people who were doing their best in trying situations.

Plymouth band, of which I was a part, regularly flew into Belfast to undertake their duties, but even then, commercial flights prohibited the carriage of weapons, so we were left *au naturel* until we were met at Belfast Airport by our Commando brethren escort. Arriving wide-eyed and expecting the worst, on my first visit the band were discreetly welcomed at the airport by our Royal Marines escort, dressed, it seems, in their civilian rig of the day, consisting of tweed jackets and flat caps. Just why they all chose to dress like gamekeepers is still a mystery to me as they stuck out at the airport like nuns in a brothel, but they probably knew best.

The band were quickly ushered into the back of a fleet of Sherpa commercial delivery vans, which had the windows covered with flattened-out crisp boxes in an attempt to hide the contents, or in this case, terrified passengers. The reason we were particularly terrified on this journey was that our armed escort informed us that a number of police uniforms had recently been stolen. This meant a palpable rise in tension at every police checkpoint as our escort discretely prepared their weapons in case of ambush, and the band members rocked gently back and forth in the back of the vans praying to gods (various: one for the praying of) that these would be genuine coppers, which luckily for all concerned, they were.

For a short portion of this trip, we were housed in that noisy funhouse known as Bessbrook Mill. As well as being fortified accommodation, the foreboding mill was also a helicopter operating base, used for moving personnel around and taking troops out into the country for patrols. Apparently, it was always part of the plan that the band would be flying out into bandit country to entertain the troops in the field and it sounds just as crazy writing this forty years on as it did when the plan was revealed to the band that morning. With the Wessex helicopter blades still turning and burning, a small group of musicians ran across the pad to the waiting choppers. Needlessly ducking the rotating blades turning high above us, drums, trumpets, saxophones and other musical accoutrements were hastily thrown aboard, much to the amusement of the pilots and air crewman. There then followed a low-level wild rollercoaster of a ride, until an operational landing of sorts saw us deposited in a fortified camp somewhere in South Armagh. Welcomed by a tired-looking regimental sergeant major, who was both surprised and somewhat perturbed to see us, we were ushered into a common mess room while the helicopters hastily took off, leaving us behind. It seemed that a signal advising the RSM of our arrival had only just preceded our touching down on the helipad, along with orders to the effect that 'they are to entertain you'. So, with not the best of grace, the RSM had to go around the various rooms and wake tired Marines from their well-earned sleep, and tell them to muster in the mess room, 'where bandy will entertain you'! We set up to play as tired and grubby looking Marines, some still with camouflage cream on their faces, slowly wandered into the room. None of us who were there that day can really explain the surreal situation in which we found ourselves. The band going through the motions of playing music and *entertaining* – something that is normally well received – with the captive audience of surprised Marines blinking unbelievably at what was occurring and depriving them of much needed sleep. I think to everyone's relief we cut the programme short and a signal was sent for the helicopters to return and collect us, the pilots still laughing as they touched down. As we lifted off we looked down at the scowling face of the RSM seeing us off, wondering how he was going to explain this to his men – that is, assuming RSMs ever need to explain anything to their men. If you were one of those hapless unfortunates, dragged from your pit to listen a jazzed-up version of the 'Colonel Bogey March', please accept my apologies.

Other notable duties during those times included going into schools to play for children. Whilst these were generally well received, and more what we were used to, the politics, religious segregation and attitudes of some of the older kids could still be felt when trying to engage with them. It was not helped when, during a piece of Latin music called 'Si Si Si Trocadero', as always, we gave the children shaking percussion instruments to play along with us. The mood was somewhat spoiled when we issued a long, hollow tube-shaped guiro to a child, who then held it like a machine gun and pretended to mow down the band. We were not sure it was his politics, his sense of humour or his judging of the band's performance, but

'Members of Plymouth band playing in Belfast town centre during one of their many visits.

sometimes it best not to ask these questions lest you not like the answer. On another occasion, someone (who are these good people who make these bad decisions?) decided it would be a good idea to have the band play in the middle of Belfast town centre. Arriving in green working uniform, wearing green berets (the Band Service did in those days) and bulky flak jackets, the band nervously performed a complete one-hour programme of music in about forty minutes, before the final note and a new world record was set for packing up and getting back on the bus. Such was the urgency to 'get out of Dodge', some of the clarinet players helped carry the drum kit – something previously unheard of!

Despite the light-hearted tone to disguise our concerns about the trips, there were some enjoyable musical engagements, and we did on occasion entertain some of the right people in the right places, but like everyone else in a uniform of that era, we were not there by choice and were not always welcomed.

Some band members even did enough time in the province to receive their Northern Ireland medals – something a Marine or soldier who did lengthy tours might call in Latin '*qui accipit ius meum nasum*' ('that gets right up my nose') – but like our wearing of green berets of that time, the medals were issued and worn in accordance with Queen's Regulations.

There might be readers whose only experience of the RMBS is through this book, so I feel this is the place for a brief explanation of why the Band Service of that time wore the coveted green beret without doing the full Commando course at CTCRM. During the Second World War, Marines on ships wore a blue beret with the Globe & Laurel cap badge, which also included the bands serving on ships. In the post-war era, the green beret was issued to all trained ranks, no matter what their role or specialist training, so once again, under Queen's Regulations, the Band Service were issued with and wore green berets once they completed their junior training and passed into adult service. In the following years, with the Commando ranks earning their green berets over many months of hard work at the Commando Training Centre, it must have been increasingly irksome to see the band wearing their berets on military training courses and when deployed. Eventually, sense prevailed and in the mid-1990s, regulations were changed and the Band Service reverted to wearing blue berets, salving the conscience of the musicians and the angst of the Commandos. No one who has served at CTCRM and seen what 'Royal' goes through to earn his green beret would deny that this was the right decision and taken for all for the right reasons. I hope that puts that matter to rest.

Finally, it would be remiss to write about the troubles of Northern Ireland without touching upon the RMBS suffering their own terrorist attack at the Royal Marines School of Music in Deal. On 22 September 1989, for reasons best known to the terrorists of the Provisional IRA (PIRA), the music school and barracks at Deal was deemed a suitable target to make its political point. Deal barracks was the softest of targets, housing the school where young musicians were trained and the staff band, all of whom were engaged in just making music. With little in the way of physical protection, other than a perimeter wall and the employment of civilian security guards, gaining access to the barracks would not prove to be a problem for any determined bomber. Overnight on 21/22 September, with a team of three holed up in a nearby terraced property, one of them gained access and a bomb was placed in an area where the staff band musicians gathered each morning. With no warnings given and being timed to kill and injure the maximum number of personnel, the explosion ripped through the area causing a major collapse of the main building. The attack caused the death of eleven fine musicians on the day but both physically and mentally injured many more who suffered in the months and years following the cowardly attack. The town of Deal was also deeply affected by the attack and even though the barracks is now closed, that sad event is still remembered in the town. A suitable memorial bandstand sits on the seafront and an annual service at the memorial garden commemorates the losses of that terrible day in 1989, when musicians were needlessly murdered for a political goal. As a matter of respect and of record, here are the names of the eleven musicians murdered that day:

Musician Michael Ball	B/Cpl Andy Cleatheroe	B/Cpl Trevor Davis
Musician Richard Fice	Musician Richard Jones	B/Cpl David McMillan
Musician Chris Nolan	B/Cpl Dean Pavey	Musician Mark Petch
Musician Tim Reeves	Musician Bob Simmonds	

As a postscript to the above, during my second career in the police, I had cause to revisit Northern Ireland and work with the Royal Ulster Constabulary. My personal security concerns had not overly changed in the intervening years, and were not eased when, out socially with them after work, each of them was armed and one was always watching the pub door ready to react. Given the Good Friday Agreement and relative peace, I do hope it is different there now, for everyone's sake.

Chapter Seventeen

The Falklands: Operation Corporate

In the spring of 1982, the Argentine ruling government, a junta made up of military leaders, decided they were so unpopular with their own people that they would invade the Falkland Islands and make themselves heroes. However, in doing so, the junta had made several mistakes, not least of which was starting a process that would lead to the operational deployment of The Band of Her Majesty's Royal Marines, Commando Forces, Plymouth. As I was actually one of the band members deployed, this chapter will have a different style and voice to it as I try to write objectively and tell the story in a succinct manner, lest it become a mini Falklands book. Having already written a complete published book (*The Band That Went to War*) about our small but important contribution to the Falklands operation, you might imagine writing just a chapter would prove easier, but surprisingly, this was not the case. Condensing 70,000 words and pictures down into one chapter proved more difficult than I imagined, but I have hopefully still captured the flavour of that deployment and not cheated the reader, and this will perhaps prompt you to seek out my other book if you want to delve deeper.

Based in Stonehouse, Plymouth, the 1982 Commando Forces band was a great place to be for a young musician. Plenty of good music engagements and a couple of foreign trips each year kept the band happy, so it came of something of a surprise to be recalled from Easter leave and told we were going off to war. The reason the band were seen as essential was one of manpower and, on paper at least, their designated wartime role. As the UK and NATO were at that time still engaged in the Cold War with Russia, the Western forces were ranged to defend against mass Russian tanks and accompanying infantry sweeping across the plains into Europe. NATO forces trained for the possibility of nuclear, biological or chemical (NBCD) attacks to bolster any Russian advance. In peacetime training, the band's role was to decontaminate the battlefield wounded from any of the NBCD contaminants before they were sent into the operating theatres, where they could be treated without contaminating the doctors. As I have mentioned in a previous chapter, it might sound complicated but it mostly meant dousing the patient in Fuller's earth, an inert grey, fine powder to absorb and remove whatever agent was present. 'Bang, blot, rub' was the routine known to all servicemen of that era, as well as eating a

Canberra, now a troopship, heads slowly out of Southampton.

biscuit while wearing a gas mask and how learning defecating drills in a clumsy NBCD suit could save your life!

During our annual training with the Royal Navy Medical Squadron, the band endured the week away from music with a wry smile and typical bandy humour. Our contribution and work ethic did not go unnoticed, so when the Medical Squadron was given orders to deploy to The Falklands, the band was quickly mobilised to go with them. As well as contributing a can-do attitude, the band also made up around forty men – a manpower number that simply could not be left behind – so the band was going to war! Luckily for all concerned, we were not going alone but as part of a task force under the organisation of 3rd Commando Brigade, mostly comprising Royal Marines Commando units and elements from the Royal Navy and the British Army. We were told that we were going to Southampton to join the commandeered cruise ship *Canberra* as part of the Medical Squadron.

With thousands of Royal Marines, Parachute Regiment and an RM band heading their way, you would have thought the junta would have seen sense and left The Falklands, but juntas have their own skewed way of thinking and so it looked like the band, with some well-trained ruffians, was actually going to war.

Sailing south, the band got stuck into all manner of medical, military and physical training, as well as assisting in turning a civilian cruise liner into a troopship. Although initially told we were not to take musical instruments, our boss (Captain John Ware) decided that keeping our core skills was essential, as well as ultimately being of some benefit to the embarked troops, so our war stores looked very unusual compared to the weapons and ammunition being loaded onto *Canberra* at Southampton. It was several weeks into the voyage south before time, space and a need was found to allow the band to rehearse. It did not take long to get back into the swing of things, although playing under metal stanchions holding up the newly installed flight deck proved for interesting acoustics. As we continued with our daily military training, it became obvious that the young testosterone-fuelled Marines and Paras were becoming increasingly frustrated at the slow progress south. This boiled over into some cap badge rivalry and a few handbag-swinging bouts in the various bars around the ship. The band swung into action with a series of off-duty concerts and beat retreats to help soothe the savage beasts and ruffians of the embarked troops. I use the term 'ruffians' with a more than sneaking admiration for the training and military prowess our military possess. They were the right people for the job, but just not used to being cooped

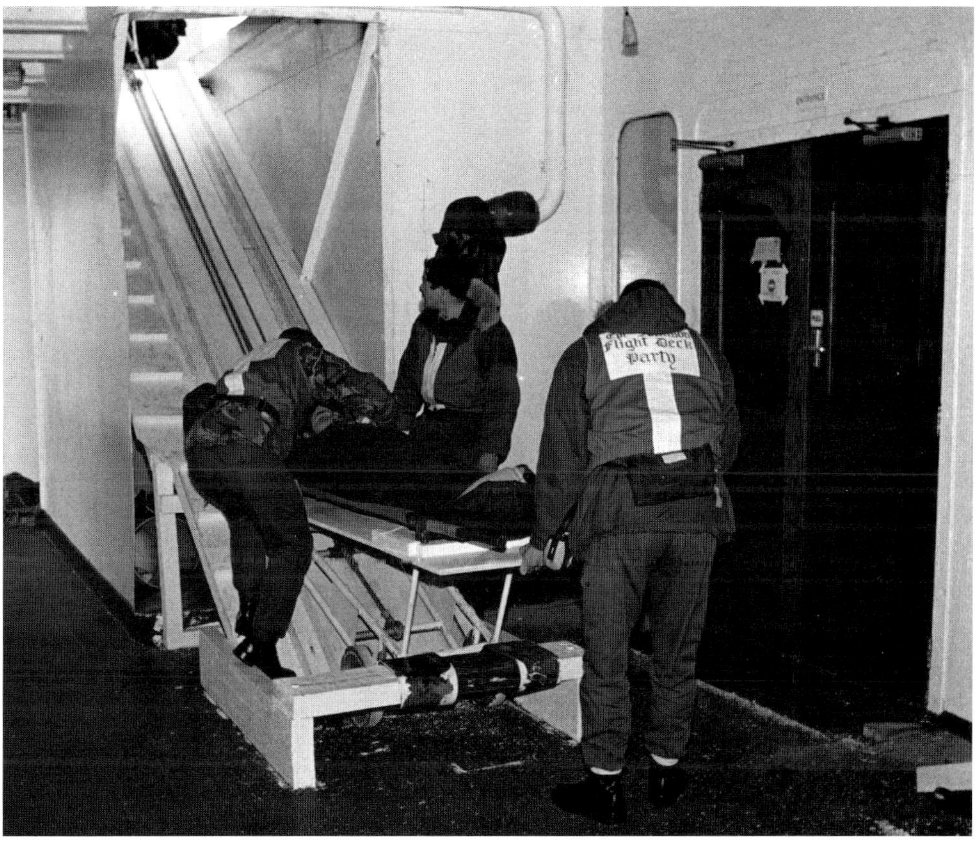

Band members practise bringing casualties down from the newly installed flight deck on *Canberra*.

up on a ship for weeks, with their hormones, physical fitness and keenness for the fight working against them, and sometimes against other persons on board with a different coloured beret!

At long last, we reached Ascension Island, where the whole of the impressive task force assembled. Once seen in its entirety, it would surely persuade the Argentines to leave peacefully before we arrived. Sadly, this was not to be and at an appropriate moment in the war timeline, one of our submarines torpedoed and sank the *General Belgrano*, followed a few days later by the sinking of HMS *Sheffield*. Knowing now we were in a shooting war, training for everyone stepped up a gear and the task force moved south with malevolent intent.

I will once again make the point that the Falklands War was indeed a war and not a conflict or any other lessening or technical description of the fighting. Yes, there are legal definitions of a war and many armchair pedants who will (and do) quote them to me. But my small part of the operations was warlike enough and when I remember what our task force at sea and ashore went through, I will stick by my own definition of what a war is. Perhaps just like love, 'war is in the eye of the beholder'. To help make my point I would refer the pedant to Russia's invasion of

The band formed a jazz quartet to get into the small bars to entertain the troops.

Ukraine, which Putin calls 'a special military operation', but there cannot be anyone who doubts it is a war in everything but name.

After training all day, during the evenings the band continued to provide some light relief and music in the form of a jazz quartet and a rock band. This enabled us to play in some of the smaller venues, including the Parachute Regiment bar, which at first caused much consternation amongst the 'Toms' until we jazzed up their regimental march, 'Ride of the Valkyries'. This gave them a reason to have some quasi-friendly rough and tumble with each other, and not us. I recall whatever it was they did, it was not fighting, dancing or singing, but a combination of all three in their inimitable airborne style!

Moving inexorably ever south, eventually we arrived at The Falklands on 21 May, which was, for us, our D-Day. The spring-like day seemed perfect as the band swung into action getting the troops to their various embarkation points for either insertion or helicopter. The band's role had suddenly changed the day before, as we were no longer going ashore with the *MASH* type medical facility but were to

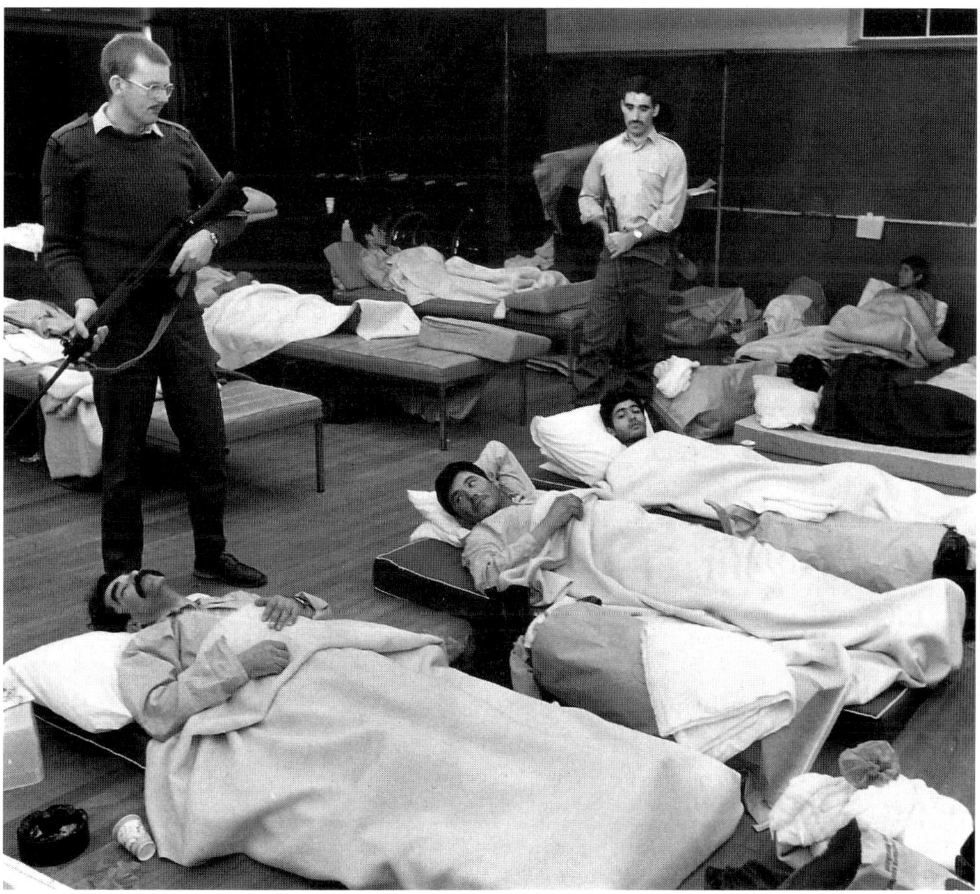

The author and another musician guarding Argentine prisoners of war.

remain as the main military unit aboard *Canberra*. Having got our troops ashore, all was going well until mid-morning, when the first of many Argentine air raids began to roar in and attack the ships around us. With a running commentary by the ship's senior naval officer telling us about incoming attacks, air raid warnings went from general to yellow and then to red in quick time, sometimes even as planes appeared and bombs were dropping. More obvious were the outgoing missiles and gunfire from our own ships towards the incoming aircraft. The chaos, noise and spectacle was frightening, as was the outgoing fire from our own weapons and those of other ships as they fought off the air attacks and brought enemy planes down. Planes exploded, ships were bombed and the band started to receive casualties onto the *Canberra* from the battles raging around them. At first we just had some Argentine walking wounded, who after being treated, were guarded by armed band members. Between air raids, we received the first of the deceased, which sadly were Royal Marines aircrew known to us, some of whom we had previously trained with. That day seemed to go on forever as the air raids continued and casualties arrived. Several of us were guarding the Argentines and the rest of the band were around the ship taking up roles vacated by the disembarked troops. In total, we undertook around forty different roles, ranging from anti-aircraft to operating octopus-like an old-fashioned wired telephone exchange. The much lauded adaptability, humour and can-do attitude of the Band Service were needed at every moment, it seemed.

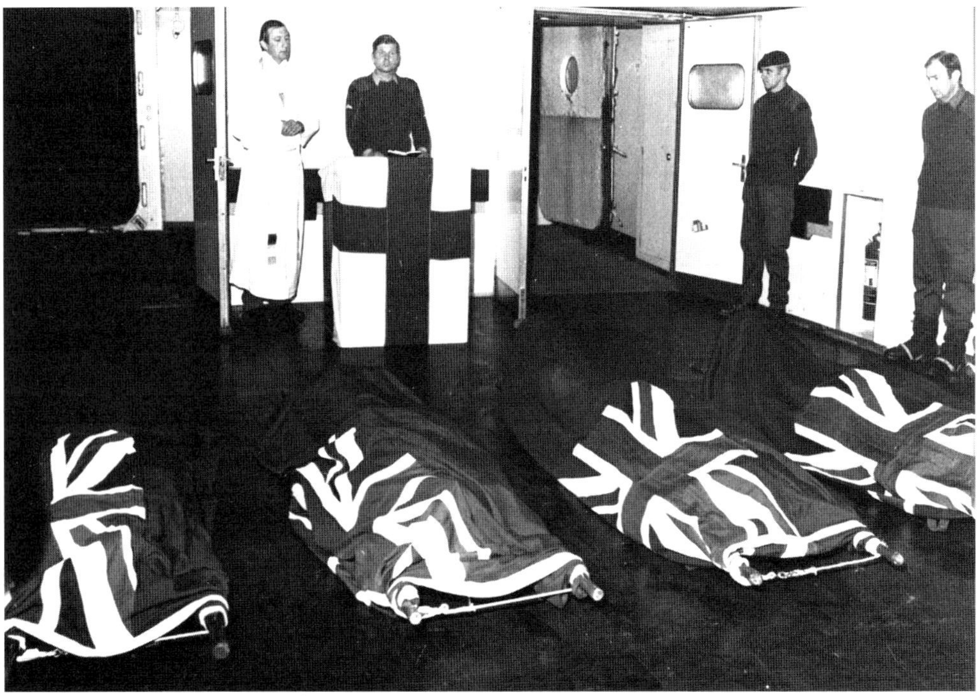

Burials at sea for our fallen warriors.

Apart from the air raids, which are always guaranteed to get your attention and become seared into your mind, one of the most visceral memories for me was taking part in burials at sea for our fallen RM comrades. While en route to collect 5 Brigade to insert them into the fight, a burial at sea service was arranged and all off-duty personnel attended. The cold, damp day, the grey sky and a large swell sweeping past the vast open door added to the sombre atmosphere as we committed the bodies of our warriors to the deep. The band provided a small brass section for the hymns and service, but it was two of our buglers (Smith and Naylor) who, with great professionalism, played the 'Last Post' in very difficult circumstances to honour our dead. It added poignancy and decorum to what was an emotionally charged but honourable service for our fallen comrades.

As the war ground on, the band worked tirelessly to accomplish all that was asked of them. We knew we were not suffering the same deprivations of our Commando brethren ashore but we had a job to do; in fact, now being the main military unit on *Canberra*, we had many jobs to do.

With the islands retaken by boots on the ground and great sacrifice at sea, after the Argentine surrender, *Canberra* was summoned into Port Stanley to take on board many thousands of Argentine POWs. Most were happy to be alive, on a cruise ship and going home; however, there were a few who tried to cause some

Musicians unloading yet more wounded from the fighting ashore.

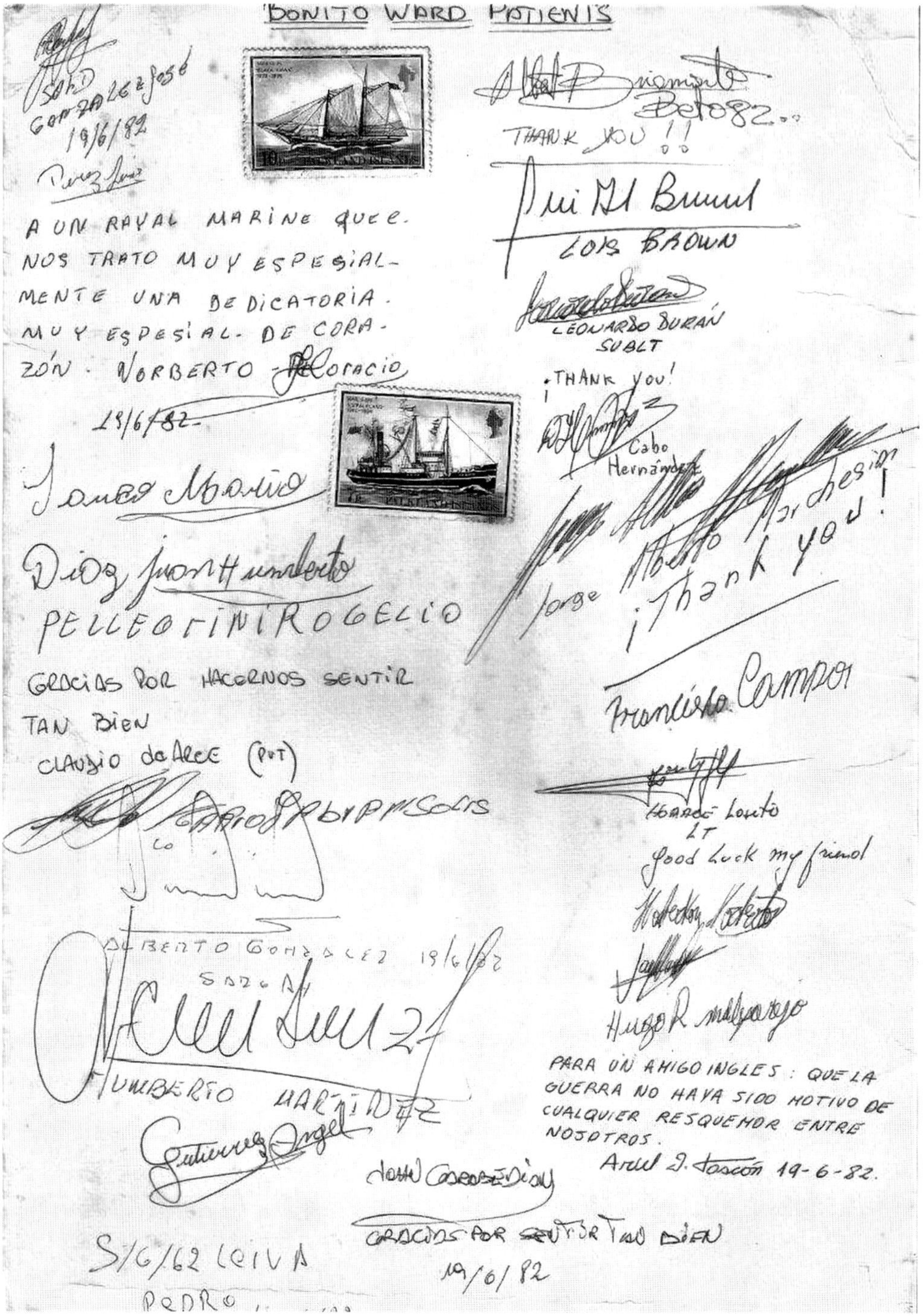

BONITO WARD PATIENTS

A UN RAYAL MARINE QUEE.
NOS TRATO MUY ESPESIAL-
MENTE UNA DEDICATORIA.
MUY ESPESIAL. DE CORA-
ZÓN. NORBERTO - HORACIO
19/6/82.

THANK YOU !!

LOIS BROWN

LEONARDO DURÁN
SUBLT

¡THANK you!

Cabo
Hernández

PELLEGRINI ROGELIO

GRACIAS POR HACERNOS SENTIR
TAN BIEN
CLAUDIO de ARCE (PVT)

¡Thank you!

Good Luck my friend

HUMBERTO MARTINEZ

PARA UN AMIGO INGLES : QUE LA
GUERRA NO HAYA SIDO MOTIVO DE
CUALQUIER RESQUEMOR ENTRE
NOSOTROS.

GRACIAS POR SENTIR TAN BIEN
19/6/82

My signed thank you card from the enemy!

trouble and they were quickly dealt with. Having had charge of one large group for a few weeks I had developed a rapport with a few of them and so before they left us in Argentina, they presented me with the most unusual war souvenir – a signed thank you card from the enemy! Was I embarrassed to receive such an unusual gift? In short, no. I had carried out my duties to the best of my abilities; the war was won and my 'customers' on both sides were happy with how I (and, of course, the band) had performed. With conflict currently raging in Ukraine and across the Israel/ Gaza border, maybe my signed card of thanks from an enemy shows there can be forgiveness and reconciliation after conflict. (Discuss.)

On the way home, the band reverted to their core skill set and played on many occasions for the troops who were now relaxing and decompressing after their trials and tribulations of being battle-tested, their training, cap badge and trust in each other having seen them through to victory. There was something of a party atmosphere around the decks of *Canberra*, but it was also tinged with sadness as we remembered that not everyone who had sailed south with us was now sailing north for home. After a couple of weeks at sea, at long last we turned into the English Channel and the naval tradition of 'Up Channel Night' was performed. The Royal Navy has a way of doing this on its ships returning home, and we were not going to let this opportunity pass us by. On a flight deck surrounded by thousands of Royal Marines, the band carried out their last official function of the operation

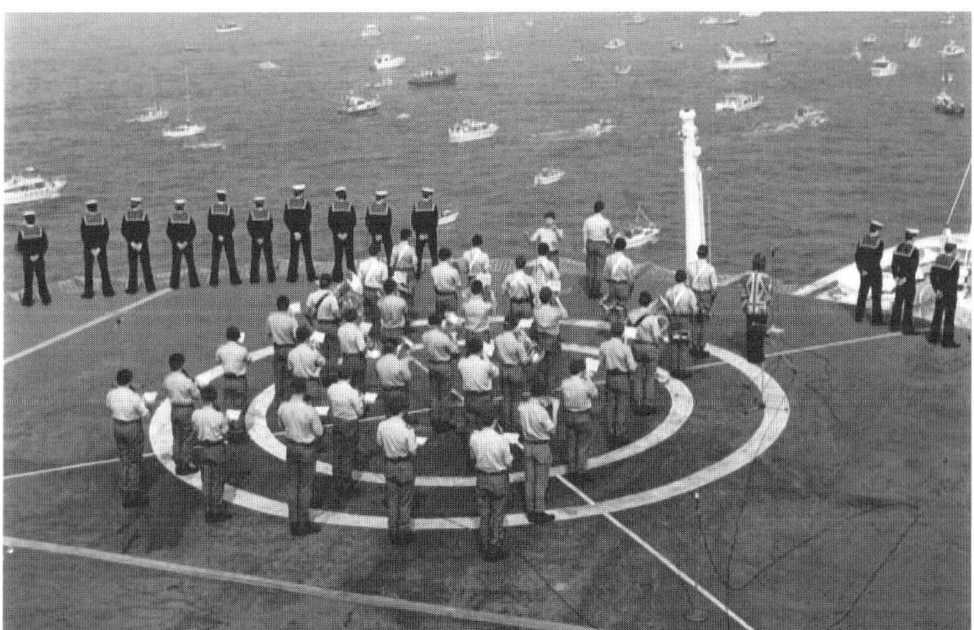

The band take pride of place on the flight deck for their last duty, as *Canberra* finally sails into her home port of Southampton.

by performing a full Beating Retreat ceremony, complete with 'Sunset' and 'Rule Britannia'. It was an emotional end to Operation Corporate, as every one of the thousands of young (and old) Marines sang their hearts out to these traditional tunes. I can imagine people on the Cornish coast off our port bow must have heard it, although the strong wind, which also caused moist eyes, might have kept it away. The next day we docked in Southampton to a fantastic reception and some well-earned leave, before reverting from the band that went to war back to musicians doing what we loved.

As I suggested at the start of this chapter, it was surprisingly the most difficult to write as at first it seemed impossible to condense a whole book down to size. However, if it has piqued your interest, then I am going to suggest you might like to seek out my dedicated book about the experiences of Commando Forces band during Operation Corporate. It has won an award or two, been readily received, with many positive reviews, but more importantly, it is a record of the Commando Forces bands' work and commitment during Operation Corporate in the spring of 1982.

Chapter Eighteen

Kosovo: Operation Agricola

In 1998, a short but vicious war sprang up in the Balkan region of Europe. On one side was Serbia and Montenegro, and on the other the Kosovo Liberation Army (KLA) backed by Albania. The war only lasted two years but was so vicious in its nature that both the United Nations and NATO got involved, which in turn led to the deployment of British Armed Forces under the joint banner of KFOR (Kosovo Force). What prompted such a strong response from the international community was the *alleged* purely ethnic cleansing of the Albanians, and I use the word alleged for legal reasons and, since I was not there, balance. What is not in doubt is that many thousands of people died and there were horrendous pictures of mass killings and pictures of Nazi-style concentration camps, which eventually brought NATO into the war and KFOR into existence.

Although bombing Serbian targets from the air was the main *modus operandi*, boots on the ground were also needed to operate as a peacekeeping force, leading to many countries of NATO contributing military personnel. The politics and diplomacy in this conflict are as convoluted as the anger and hate that ran through it. As I am fond of saying, I am not a historian, so if you have a need to know more about the overall Kosovo War, then Mr Google is your friend and there are also many books on the subject. What I can say for sure is that at the height of its contribution, the UK had around 19,000 troops on the ground, and as the title of this book suggests, some of them were Royal Marines musicians.

The first cohort of musicians heading for Kosovo were, surprisingly, all volunteers, and each would have had their own reason for putting their name forward. I had to volunteer to go to the Falklands War, for a reason I think was born out of naivety and youth, which today is called FOMO (fear of missing out).

Formed under the uninspired title of K Band, the group was sent to CTCRM for an intensive period of military refresher training. My respondents noted that this was taken far more seriously than in previous military training periods and culminated in a week living in the field and a three-day training and testing phase at a United Nations training facility, which probably accounts for the way the training was undertaken. The training was also notable as it required the senior non-commissioned officers (sergeants and above) to undertake a study in post-traumatic stress disorder (PTSD), so that they could identify just what the people under them were going through and, perhaps more importantly, how they were coping with it. At this point, some of the volunteers were starting to wonder what they had let themselves in for!

Having completed their training, passed their tests and deemed fit for active service, K Band were flown into the Kosovo theatre of operations aboard an RAF C-130 Hercules. If you have not flown in a Hercules then I can tell you they are as noisy as they look, with uncomfortable canvas seats the length of the aircraft, the effect heightened by operational and tactical steep approaches to airfields to minimise exposure to enemy fire. Add to that the obligatory RAF in-flight ration bag containing a tin of fizzy pop, a dry and curly meat-like sandwich, and a pastry that would leave your mouth coated in grease until your next birthday, and the misery of the journey is complete.

Once established in their new camp there was first a welcome lecture, which was less about the welcome and more about the dangers they would face, not least of which would be land and anti-vehicles mines. The lecture, and the experience of those giving it, was invaluable as the band members would be heavily involved in the movement of vehicles, patients, troops and prisoners as their tour in theatre went on. As part of the Royal Navy Medical Squadron, they moved into their base, called Harden Lines, and relieved the present incumbents, the Royal Army Medical Corp (RAMC), who could now go home for well-earned leave.

An interesting note about the name of the camp is that it was named after Lance Corporal H.E. Harden, VC, of the RAMC. He was posthumously awarded the Victoria Cross during the Second World War, while operating with 45 Commando RM. The RAMC is rightly very proud of the number of Victoria Crosses earned by its members over the years, but sadly, due to the nature of its work, many are awarded posthumously to these brave men and women.

The K Band members deployed on Operation Agricola also operated under sub-operational titles of Operation Trojan and Operation Sexton, dependent on their role within the organisation. They were split into two main troops with a band sergeant in charge of each one. One of these was designated as the ambulance troop and provided three teams of personnel to drive the battlefield ambulances and support the medics in the back who would be taking care of the casualties. With a band corporal or sergeant as vehicle commander and a musician as an assisting medic, it soon became clear why such strong emphasis had been placed on first aid refresher training during their work-up period.

K Band personnel were rotated through Operation Trojan, their main job being to safely escort Serbians who needed medical treatment through Albanian areas for treatment. Another rotation saw some of the musicians involved in Operation Sexton, which supported United Nations forensics teams as they searched for evidence of

A fanfare for the grand reopening of Pristina railway station.

war crimes. An unfortunate part of these investigations required the exhuming of the dead to check for signs of torture or execution in cold blood – or murder, as the civilised world calls it. The UN teams required close guarding as they went about their duties as none of the local combatants were overly pleased to see them, the teams only getting help from those wanting to know what had happened to their own missing loved ones. The digging up of the dead was yet another Band Service job description missing from the careers brochures.

As with all the operational deployments I have experienced or researched, there always seems to be an element of 'mission creep' in the work given and then entrusted to the band ranks, as commanders recognise the skill level and abilities of the musicians under their command. Another example of this was trusting the military skills of some of the musicians to go out on patrol with Commando units and taking charge of convoys from Pristina to Greece as convoy commanders.

One of the respondents to my call for information of the operation was Bugler Charlie Williams. Like me, do not be fooled by the name, as Charlie Williams is not only a female, she has the honour and distinction of being the first female to ever join the Royal Marines Buglers Branch. Charlie recalls one of the higher risk parts of the operation was transferring prisoners by road through areas where the enemy lived, and that they would not have wanted to break down in the 'badlands' carrying such an unwelcomed passenger. On the humanitarian side, she and another of the band, Emma Thorne, organised a teddy bear appeal and collection, the stuffed toys being distributed fairly around the local children in need, disregarding any of the religious or political divides.

Another of my Kosovo respondents was the then Bugler (currently Warrant Officer 1 RM) Phil Hawkins. Although very young in service, having only passed out of training in April of 1999, he and fellow squad mate Bugler Stu Warmington were tasked with playing a herald trumpet fanfare to mark the reopening of the main railway station in Pristina. Along with other in-theatre buglers of a similar young age and service, they also led a parade through Pristina, presumably to 'fly the NATO flag' and show that life can still have some normality to it, even if that normality means waking the town with three beat rolls and a rousing drum solo.

Some of Phil Hawkins' other memories include medical and guarding support to the Medical Squadron, attending road traffic accidents and even playing the 'Last Post' at the British Embassy in Skopje, Macedonia: have bugle, will travel, it seems. On the subject of travel, Phil's admin may be as unreliable as mine, as due to a misunderstanding, he left Kosovo for his two-week rest and recuperation leave a week before he should have. With his return flight already booked, he found himself the beneficiary of a week's extra leave and was very chilled and relaxed when he eventually returned. The 'chilled and relaxed' soon left him when a prank was played on him, telling him he was going to be the subject of the very serious formal charge of absent without leave (AWOL). Having lost several pounds in weight sweating it out over a twenty-four hour period, the joke was eventually broken and Phil 'the chill' could breathe easily again.

As with all modern deployments, music was never far from the minds of the musicians and between long hours and shifts, they somehow managed to keep up their musical skills. In their spare time, they played for the international troops in their locale, providing a concert band, a marching band, a rock band and even a dance band for people to tap a foot or shake a trotter, so at least to temporarily forget that they were in a war zone. Music is also an important tool in the 'hearts and minds' campaign to win over a local population, and the band were utilised many times playing for the locals and providing them with some respite from the war they were living in. There will be some young Kosovans whose earliest memories will be of their first teddy bear or hearing their first drum solo, but without any idea by whom they were supplied. Well done Royal!

Chapter Nineteen

Iraq: Operation Granby

In 1990, the Middle East once more became a place of unrest when the leader of Iraq, Saddam Hussein, decided he would invade the neighbouring country of Kuwait. His reasons were convoluted and varied, depending on which of his speeches you listened to, but in essence, it was a land grab to seize assets and capture his wealthy neighbours' oil fields. There were, are, and will be invasions of other countries that go either unnoticed or diplomatically ignored for political reasons, but this one was very much noticed, not least, because it involved oil and affected the world dollar price of oil per barrel. This potential oil crisis got the Americans' attention, as it did many other Middle Eastern Gulf states, and some took umbrage at one Arab country invading another. But Saddam Hussein had a thick skin to offset such umbrage and it would take much more than words to shift him.

As you can imagine, there were lots of quiet diplomatic efforts, back-door political pressures and open military threats made to get Iraq to withdraw from Kuwait, all of which came to nothing. The Americans, with a very difficult political balancing act, eventually put together a military coalition force to back up the threats, which the United Kingdom signed up to. With the Americans calling it Operation Desert Storm, the British went for the less demonstrative and understated title of Operation Granby. Gearing up for military action war in the Middle East involving all three services, it only took the military planners a short time to realise that if the UK was going to war, then a Royal Marines band would also be needed, so the Commander-in-Chief Fleet band was put on notice to deploy.

Sending a small advance party onto RFA *Argus*, initially the band were designated as medical orderlies, but as you will have read in other chapters, any band deployed can expect to undertake a wide range of other roles and responsibilities not written in any operational order, and then at the end of the day, still be required to play music.

By the time of this Middle Eastern war crisis, the Director of Music from the Falklands War, John Ware had risen from the rank of captain to the lofty heights of lieutenant colonel and Principal Director of Music Royal Marines. From his personal service stemming back to HMS *Centaur*, through the Falklands War and beyond, John Ware had some idea of what could be expected of the band. He wrote at the time:

RFA *Argus* at sea.

> Engaged primarily as medical orderlies they will also be active in a musical capacity, providing the invaluable morale and psychological support which only a band can. Once again, as in the Falklands campaign in 1982, the Band Service has the opportunity to prove that even in modern times, there remains a need for a group of able musicians who are also intelligent and flexible enough to adapt quickly and efficiently to any task that may present itself.

Wise words from someone who had already 'been there' many times during his Band Service career and now, as the head of the Band Service for that period, offered advice and leadership.

At the other end of the Band Service rank structure, young musician Chris Piggin, a euphonium and cello player, had just been transferred from Britannia Royal Naval College Band RAF Northolt, where the Royal Marines Band of the Commander-in-Chief (CIC) was situated. With time for some leave, he had taken himself on a tour around North Africa and Europe. While in Rabat in Morocco, he saw the headlines about Saddam Hussein's invasion of Kuwait, but aged just 22, and with the innocence of youth on his side, he assumed it would have no impact on his life and career; and like many young musicians before him, he would be proved wrong. After arriving back at Northolt and joining his new band, he was summoned by the boss, Captain Mick Goss, Director of Music. Chris was told his first job with the band was a 'nice little jolly' to Gibraltar, so having just unpacked from Dartmouth, he repacked and crated his uniforms and instruments onto a lorry destined for an RAF flight to Gibraltar. As luck, or military unluck, would have it, within the hour the band were all gathered together in the band room to hear an announcement from the DOM. Just like musicians before them, me included, they listened in silence as their boss gave them a warning order that some of them would be going to war and a decision on who would be forthcoming later that day. At that point, Chris blinked and took stock of his life choices. As he had just arrived in the band and felt safe in the knowledge that his kit was on its way to Gibraltar, he felt sure that he could not possibly be picked for the war. It seems that, once again, self-assuredness was no shield against the exigencies of the service, and so he was proven wrong; by the end of the day he was unloading his gear from the lorry and repacking his kit to deploy on RFA *Argus*.

Other urgent band administrative matters had to be undertaken quickly as the order from above required fifty of the band under a bandmaster to deploy. Their Director of Music, Captain Mick Goss, recognised the size of this deployment really needed a commissioned officer, along with another warrant officer, so Peter Best, who had already been earmarked for higher rank, was made Acting Warrant Officer 2 Bandmaster for the duration. Peter Best, known for his fine violin playing and musicianship, also served aboard the Royal Yacht and would eventually finish his career as a commissioned major and Director of Music RM.

The band personnel selected for deployment were given a short weekend leave to see their families and make any necessary personal arrangements. They were then sent to Portsmouth for a brief and intense period of training, which included ship's firefighting, weapons training, nuclear, biological and chemical decontamination and important refresher in-depth first aid training. There was an added bonus in having a former Falklands veteran in the band training alongside them. Musician Fred Millar had been on the hospital ship *Uganda* throughout the Falklands War and was able to offer first-hand accounts of what he had seen in that conflict, and what they could expect this time around. It was both frightening and reassuring, depending on which part of his experiences you dwelled upon. The FOF 3 band's Falklands War experiences aboard the SS *Uganda* are covered in a dedicated chapter in my book, *The Band That Went to War*.

With training completed, the band moved to Plymouth to join RFA *Argus*. Initial impressions that she was an 'ugly and dirty ship' did not change much as the band found their berths, which were deep within the refuse collection part of the ship! The accommodation was somewhat better for those further up the rank structure, and the newly promoted bandmaster Pete Best had no such complaints (RHIP rank has its privileges). Having just undergone a quick refit for the war, and with dockyard workers still swarming over the ship, the dust, soot and grime were everywhere, and were breathed in and tasted.

In its military role, the *Argus* was designated as a Primary Casualty Receiving Ship (PCRS), which means having different credentials and status to an official Red Cross hospital ship; it could not be afforded any protection of red crosses – not that it would have made much difference to Saddam Hussein. Quickly fitted out with more hospital facilities, a decontamination cell, an ungainly portable cabin and extra refrigeration units for the deceased, the reminders of a ship going to war were everywhere. RFA *Argus* already had quite a distinguished naval career, having served in The Falklands (as the MV Contender *Bezant*, before being renamed), and would later go on to serve in the Second Gulf War, the Bosnia War, the Kosovo War and, as you read earlier in this book, in Africa for the Ebola mission.

With the *Argus* now on a war footing and everybody busy making their own preparations, there was no meet and greet from the crew and the band were left to their own devices to settle in. Chris Piggin recalls finding the access hatch to the helicopter deck, but in the evening gloom, almost falling 15 meters down into the open aircraft lift shaft. It appears that it had become stuck and there were no safety barriers in place, almost causing young Chris to be the first victim of the Gulf War, before the ship had even left port.

The next day the Fleet Air Arm arrived in a stylish fashion, with the helicopters of the Royal Navy's 846 Squadron making a grand entrance in their newly painted desert pink camouflage choppers. The impression to the watching bandies was that it was like a scene from *Apocalypse Now*, and it took little imagination to hear the 'Ride of the Valkyries' playing over the din of the helicopters' rotor blades.

Having taken on the helicopters and extra war stores required, they sailed from Plymouth on a wet and windy October day. The band were playing on the open deck to no one in particular, as the goodbyes had already been said the previous weekend and there was seemingly little interest from the locals in Devonport. As she passed the King Billy statue marking the end of Devonport Dockyard, the ship acknowledged the salute from the Flag Officer Plymouth at Mount Wise as they sailed past, buglers on the ship and the shore sounding the alert before the salute was given and returned. It was a sombre sailing but one that would be repeated twenty-fours later as the ship had to return to Plymouth for a quick repair.

When they were eventually on their way, those first-time sailors without their sea legs suffered as the ship headed south, and then overnight entered the Bay of Biscay for a rough sea state that is informally known amongst sailors as 'Harry Roughers'. A side note is that in the Royal Navy, the word 'Harry' could help describe many things and situations by adding it as a prefix: 'Harry Sippers' if you wanted to share some of your rum ration or drink; 'Harry Goffer' to describe either a lime squash drink or a large wave hitting the ship; and 'Harry Maskers' for the ubiquitous rolls of heavy duty black tape. It might originate from a character called Harry Lime in an old film called *The 39 Steps*, but I am sure some crusty matelot will put me right. The above names have, over time, also been to used defeat natural and official justice, as ships in port have been visited by local police and females various, all demanding an interview with Marine Harry Maskers, who had left his name in a bar. I am sure you can join the dots yourself.

At sea state 'Harry Roughers', the experienced sailors smiled and stood aside as the new sailors and bandies rushed from the open deck to the heads (ship's toilets) and then back again trying to find comfort or respite in the part of the ship that was moving the least. Regardless of the sea state, the preparations and training for the forthcoming war took priority, which for some of the band members was a welcome distraction from the moving ship. The band were split into sections and given their specialist roles and areas of responsibility. Chris Piggin's allocated duty is probably best summed up in his own words:

> I was selected to work within the NBC decontamination cell. It was our job to receive the wounded, carry them to the decontamination cell, give first aid, but use copious amounts of 'Fuller's earth' where necessary, should the casualty be subjected to a chemical or biological attack.

As you can see, even then the magic Fuller's earth was still in use as the primary chemical, biological or nuclear clean-up of choice, its absorbent properties purportedly working small miracles. Whilst amazing in its simplicity and amusing in its application, there was a strong possibility that Saddam Hussein could once again use chemical agents, so you had to put your faith in your kit, training and a tan-coloured talcum powder.

As they ventured further south the weather improved and the band settled into the ship and their training regimes. They were encouraged to take part in fitness and physical training on the flight deck and also in a rudimentary gym set up in the hangar. As they trained for their different action stations and scenarios, they were required to wear anti-flash kit and overalls, and to carry their respirator, individual breathing apparatus and first aid kit with them at all times. It became cumbersome and a nuisance to be so heavily kitted out and constantly having to open and close doors and hatches, but training for war always carries that 'train hard, fight easy' mantra, which has proved its worth over the years.

Pete Best remembers the long training days dressed in complete NBCD suits and respirators, with the band carrying heavily laden stretchers around the hot deck.

There was the possibility of people fainting or, worse still, the very real danger of having a steamed-up respirator and falling down an open aircraft lift shaft.

Transiting through the Mediterranean, the band's training and hard work had paid off and they felt quite confident in what was required of them. RFA *Argus* made its way to Port Said in Egypt. I have mentioned this before but I think it is worth repeating. It is the place where, in 1956, thirteen Royal Marines were killed in the Suez conflict, one of whom was my own father, Royal Marine Brian John Short of 42 Commando Royal Marines.

Having docked in what was now a friendly port, the band and some of the crew were sent on a sightseeing trip to see the Sphinx and pyramids at Giza. It might seem strange to give personnel time off on the way to a war, but rest and recreation (R&R) are important to keep up morale amongst a hard-working crew, and with an uncertain future ahead of them it was obviously someone with an experienced mind and a thought for the welfare of the people under their command who authorised it. Another thoughtful welfare gesture was made by the ship's officers in inviting the famous Egyptian 'Lucky Lucky' men aboard the ship to sell their trinkets, perform their tricks and entertain the band and crew. There is a long tradition of the Royal Navy and indeed, most merchant vessels, of allowing these temporary entertainers on board their ship as a distraction from the daily routine. For ships and crews headed home, it also allowed the last-minute purchase of a dubious quality 'glass-beaded' gift for the loved ones at home, complete with a dodgy certificate stating how many diamond carats it was purported to be.

Having at last reached the Persian Gulf, off the coast of Oman, the band were amazed to find themselves literally in a sea of allied aircraft carriers, warships and support vessels, constantly overflown by many aircraft and helicopters on patrol. The ships and aircraft were from the many nations who had signed up to be part of the coalition against Saddam Hussein and it was hard to be impressed.

One thing that had become apparent was the lack of news and up-to-date information, with some of the newspapers and mail received being nearly two weeks old. Some of the band became involved in putting this right and, using a video camera bought ashore, Chris and his bandmates set up a daily broadcast of news and information that was received by Telex every day. This small innovation once again showed what a little musical intellect can do when it meets a problem, and the big impact a simple solution can have to morale. Pete Best became a roving news reporter, recording news and events for replay over the ship's TV system to help keep the crew informed and entertained.

Some of the band were also involved in the post office system under the title of 'Argus Air', and the movement of 'Blueys'. The Bluey was a thin, lightweight combined letter and envelope all in one, which provided a communication lifeline

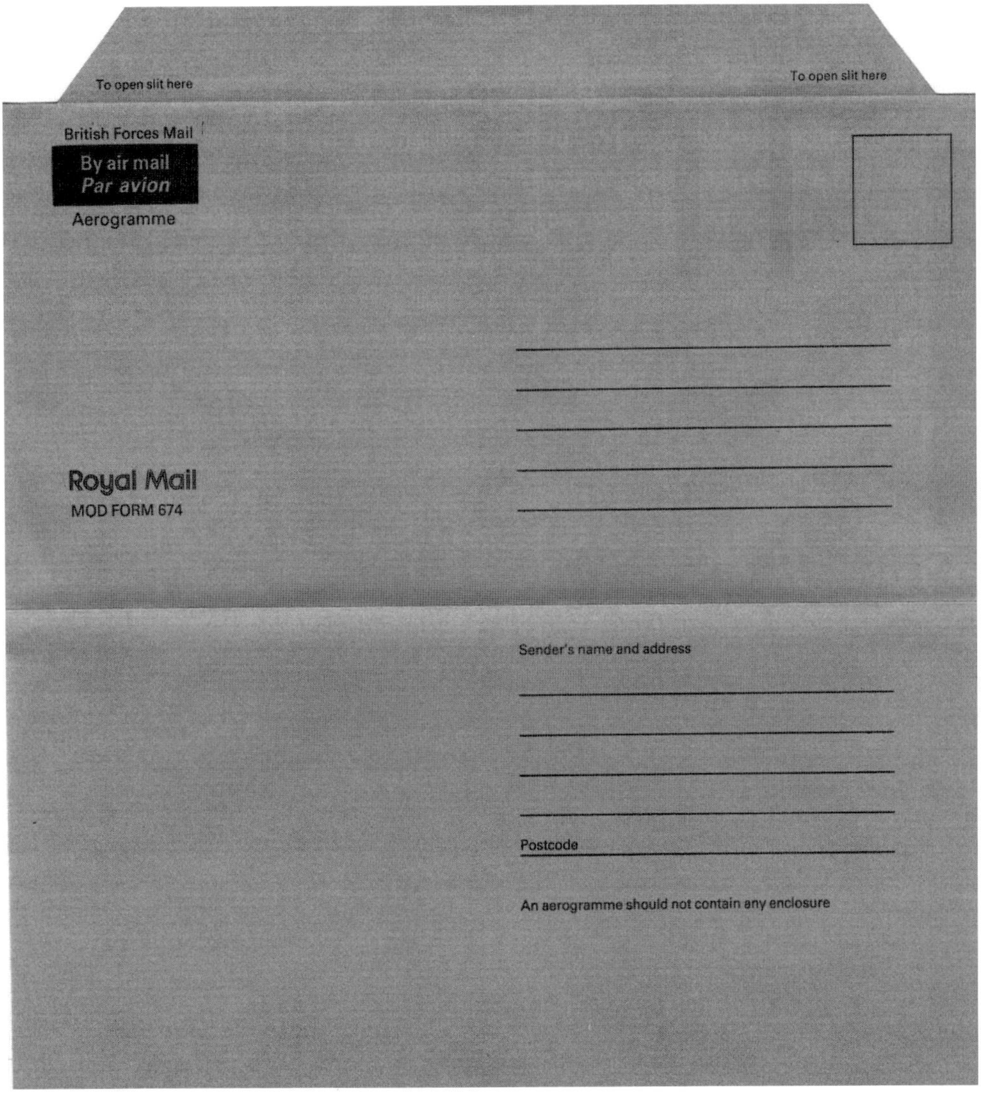

The lightweight Bluey enabled many more letters to be transported and therefore more people to be kept in touch in time of war.

between many thousands of sailors, Marines and anyone stationed away from home. Designed to cut down on weight when being flown from the UK or out to a ship by helicopter, the Bluey was another important factor in keeping up morale for those on board, and contact for those at home.

Back in the UK, as in most recent wars, some of the local newspapers ran stories on the theme of 'Our boys at war' and asked for contributions. Most of the pictures posted were of 'roughty toughty' marine types, bare chested, holding general-purpose machine guns, which suited the image the papers wanted to portray and increased unsolicited mail from females severalfold. For reasons best known only to the editor of the local newspaper in Oakham, they chose as their centrefold a picture of a fantastic young RM musician called Paul Hart. Musician Paul Hart has been described by his bandmates as a 'thoroughly lovely guy' and the epitome of what the RMBS has to offer musically and socially, but the picture used portrayed a young man that was also described by his bandmates as 'a saintly figure, looking more like a young Frank Spencer rather than Rambo'! For some reason, his 'rabbit in the headlights' pose, combined with his ungainly landing pad beret, had something of an effect on a certain demographic of Oakham. Consequently, Paul was inundated with thousands of letters, mostly from ladies who wished him well, but who also, let's say, wanted to *take care of him* in many other and exotic ways. During one long-awaited mail delivery, he personally received about 80 per cent of the mail, so much so in fact that he simply had to share some of the goodwill. So, like a priest giving away communion wafers, Paul gave away some letters to the less fortunate amongst the band. Whether it came with a laying on of hands or a blessing is not recorded and, perhaps luckily, neither are the contents of the missives.

An author's note here. So much of this band's experience echoes Commando Forces band experience during the Falklands War some eight years earlier. On the *Canberra*, we were training and adapting the ship for war, visiting odd ports en route, being amazed at the size of the enterprise we were undertaking and also the size of the task force we were a part of. Even back then we were also receiving Blueys and supportive mail from people we did not know back home. It made a huge difference then and obviously once again, to the members of Fleet band aboard *Argus*, especially to Musician Paul Hart and his newly acquired harem.

During this early assembly phase of the war, before hostilities commenced, the ships of the fleet could put into Gulf state ports for stocking up and, where possible, shore leave for the crew. RFA *Argus* was no exception, and the ship also managed several port visits in Dubai, Bahrain and Riyadh. Although these were friendly ports, a warning was given that ships in port could be vulnerable to attack from sympathisers and agents of Iraq, so port visits also included twenty-four-hour armed security duties for some of the band members. During one such guard duty, Chris Piggin was armed, alert and wary of not letting anything happen on his watch. At about 6 am, while patrolling the rear deck, he became aware of bubbles appearing on the surface of the water and realised at once there must be a diver down there. Having not been briefed on friendly force divers, and fearing this could be a sabotage attempt, as the bubbles increased Chris raised his rifle and took aim at where the diver would appear. In a flurry of bubbles and equipment, the diver surfaced exactly where predicted and glancing upwards found himself looking up the barrel of a rifle. Now at the wrong end of a rifle with a musician at the other who was shouting at him to 'HALT!', the onus was on the diver to explain the who, where and why of the situation. Quickly removing his mask and breathing tube, the desperate diver shouted: 'I'M ONE OF YOURS, I'M CHECKING FOR MINES FOR CHRIST SAKE!' Chris Piggin was greatly relieved to hear this explanation and with his heart still pounding in his chest at what had nearly transpired, took a moment to reflect and gather his thoughts. Why nobody had thought to mention at the guards' security briefing the important detail that the ship was sending down divers to check for mines is not known, or at least not admitted to, but it led to a very tense standoff between the diver and the musician. Given that you will have read above that Chris very nearly became the first casualty of the war, he also came very close to firing the first offensive shot!

With the war not due to 'kick off' until sometime in the New Year, the ship prepared itself as best it could for some sort of Christmas celebration. The ship's 'Bish' (chaplain) organised a Christmas carol concert and the band supplied members to play for the assembled throng. Being in a hot country at Christmas, well away from home and loved ones, was strange to those experiencing life in a blue suit for the first time, but for the old salts it was business as usual. One of the novel ways to make Christmas feel more like Christmas, was the tossing of chemical tube lights. When snapped, the chemicals inside the plastic tubes were mixed and produced different coloured lights. Once thrown over the side, they created a mystical and faintly Christmassy feel as the lights floated on the waves. Just how this related to a birth in a manger 2,000 years previously might not be clear to the reader, but it was all they had. Some of the band were flown around other ships in the fleet to play Christmas carols, and enjoyed the festivities on each ship as they did so. Resulting from the many ships' visits, one band member claimed three Christmas dinners in one day!

Chris also had a thriving enterprise in recording the band and crew's Christmas messages on video tape to be sent home. Getting creative, he played emotional Christmas music while they spoke to their loved ones via the video camera. His description is quite touching:

> I had people sitting in front of the camera with 'I'm Dreaming of a White Christmas' playing in the background for added effect. I have never witnessed so many grown, gung-ho males broken down to tears so easily. For some of them we had to do the messages without the music in the background, because otherwise they could not get through it.

It is easy to imagine the emotional combination of being away from home, heading to war and trying to send normal Christmas messages to family back home.

Another unusual occurrence happened when the ship was visited by TV magician Paul Daniels. Famous for his wit, magic tricks and badly fitting wigs, the late Paul Daniels (formerly of the RAF) was greatly appreciated for making the journey to the Middle East and performing on *Argus* and other ships. Did he enjoy it? 'Not a lot,' which, for you young enough not to have known him, was Paul Daniels' catchphrase.

With the brief holiday festivities over, thoughts once again returned to the impending war. One of the band started a sweepstake, with everyone chipping in some money and picking the lucky (or unlucky) date they thought the war would start. The winner who chose 17 January was our very own contributor Chris Piggin; it seems that at last his luck was changing.

When they were back at sea, the band once more settled into the ship's routine, taking part in more emergency drills, action stations and more advanced medical training. They did, as all RMBS members had done before them, find time to keep up their musical skills and play for some of the ship's officers and crew, but primarily their time was spent preparing for war, which was now looking ever more likely.

Since the Falklands War some eight years previously, the Royal Navy had started to take the idea of post-traumatic stress disorder rather more seriously, and so the band and crew were exposed to various films, lectures and discussions on what to expect and how best to deal with it. RN psychiatrists were available to talk to and Pete Best recalls the useful relaxation techniques they were taught back then; he still uses them now when he feels the need to switch off and relax.

It was 17 January when the war began, with a huge armada of aircraft of many nations starting the attacks on the Iraqi air force and airfield infrastructure. It was hoped that this massive show of force would lead to Saddam Hussein backing down and withdrawing from Kuwait, but in the way of all despots, tyrants and military juntas he refused, believing that he could either win or, by bringing Israel into the war, cause the break-up of the coalition and force an escalation of the war. Those on the upper deck of HMS *Argus* could hear and feel the reverberations of the bombardments taking place as the many hundreds of coalition planes and ships began their attacks.

During this phase of the war, worrying reports reached the ship and home about the mounting RAF's Tornado low-level bomber losses that were taking their toll on RAF aircraft and crews. Generally regarded as a good aircraft by the crews, with its sophisticated Terrain-following radar (TFR), the Iraq War would be the first battle test for the airframe and the much-vaunted JP223 weapon, a low-level runway-cratering munition. The Tornado, the crews and the JP223 all worked as advertised, but the delivery method of flying straight down the enemy's runways meant putting the aircraft into a maelstrom of airfield anti-aircraft missiles and surface-to-air missile fire, resulting in the loss of several crews and aircraft before a different method of delivery was used. I mention this detail, as in RAF Navigator John Nichol's excellent book *Tornado*, he writes that when he was shot down on such a mission, he ejected and found himself in an expanse of desert. With his billowing orange parachute and survival box, he says, 'I could not have felt more conspicuous if I had a Royal Marines Band with me!' He might well have written RAF band, but somehow chose the RM Band to make his point, which I think we will take as a compliment of sorts.

Another interesting point John Nichol made in his book concerns how following the mounting Tornado losses, the RAF senior officers agreed to a change of tactics. Referring to 'the White Cliff of Dover' syndrome, when Second World War pilots bravely defended the UK in the Battle of Britain, the attrition rates and losses back then were accepted as they were defending their homeland. Now they found themselves in the Middle East fighting someone else's war and asked themselves if it was worth dying for or whether they should change tactics and take a safer option and weapon delivery method. Perhaps this is outside the remit of this book, but I include it as thought-provoking for anyone who has or who might find themselves in a similar position one day, taking on an enemy who is fighting for *their* homeland, with the added impetus and commitment that brings to their fight.

On 17 January, as the war started, *Argus* sounded her ship's emergency alarms and the band and crew 'turned to' their action stations, donning their anti-flash suits and hoods. With the Iraqi Air Force being pounded relentlessly, but on occasion still trying to fight the technically superior coalition aircraft, the air threat to HMS *Argus* was limited but very real, which manifested itself four times in one day. Having already 'turned to' and at action stations, the crew and band were horrified to hear over the ship's PA system: 'STANDBY, STANDBY, BRACE, BRACE, BRACE.' This is generally bad news and, given just before a bomb or missile attack on a ship and speaking from experience, it certainly gets your attention as you wait for the bang. By divine intervention, or more likely the intervention of an American F15 pilot, the threat was taken out and the ship was not hit. Another 'STANDBY, PREPARE FOR BRACE' did have a real and deadly threat to it as an Iraqi missile was detected heading for the fleet's location, but that missile was detected by a British warship and taken out before it could present a danger to *Argus* and the rest of the fleet.

With the war well underway, also came the real possibility of a retaliatory chemical attack from Iraq, something that Saddam Hussein had done before and now threatened the coalition forces with, so gas masks were now worn, adding to the already worrying and uncomfortable situation. All the band and crew were now closed up in their action stations, clothed from head to foot in anti-flash gear and sucking in air through their respirators, waiting for information about attacks to come through on the ship's PA system. All things considered, it was a very stressful time for all concerned … but when is war not so?

With the allied coalition forces having achieved air superiority, they opened another front attacking Iraq's ground forces. This new phase of the war, with a diminished air threat, saw *Argus* remaining at sea for around a month, much of the time in something of a communications blackout. Official Telex and radio traffic was still getting through, but due to circumstances or, as the military describes it, 'exigencies of the service', mail and other lines of communication were cut off. They did hear that, in desperation, Saddam Hussein had taken to firing long-range missiles into coalition airbases, and also into Israel in the hope of widening the war by dragging them into the conflict, but so far he had been unsuccessful and was quickly losing the war.

With this change in direction ashore, the band's duties aboard the *Argus* had now taken another turn with the added responsibility of ship's lookouts. The reason many more hands and eyes were now needed on deck was because of the danger of sea mines. Set off magnetically, acoustically or the traditional, time-honoured method of running into them, regardless of which, all produced the same results: a big bang. The mines had been dropped liberally into the ocean to target coalition ships, or indiscriminately any ship that might hit them. Two American ships operating close to *Argus* struck mines and were damaged. The two vessels, the helicopter carrier USS *Tripoli* and the guided-missile cruiser USS *Princeton*, were already engaged in minesweeping, but even with all the available technology of the time, both were still hit. Both ships suffered substantial structural damage, but officials declared 'they remained ready for warfare, and casualties were light'. *Argus* avoided hitting any mines, so perhaps the Americans should have opted for 'bandies with binoculars' instead of relying on technology.

One of the American casualties from a mine explosion was flown onto *Argus* for treatment. Taken from the helicopter down to the hospital on the ship, the sailor told of his lucky escape. Having been blown out of his shoes by the explosion, his unplanned flight avoided lower extremity damage, only to smash his head open on the bulkhead (ceiling), causing a nasty gash that needed treatment. As the first official casualty to christen the *Argus*'s hospital, he received the full attention of the medical staff before being flown back to his ship. Other mines did cause some damage to the fleet as well as a small number of injuries.

As if being told there were explosive mines in the water was not a good enough reason to be vigilant when on lookout duties, the damage and casualties of the nearby American ships certainly was. Scanning the sea and paying close attention to every bit of floating debris was called out and passed for action to the officers on the bridge. Perhaps it was this intense focus on the task in hand that brought the lookouts' attention to many other objects in the water, some that were not mines or other debris, but human bodies. At the start of the war, Iraq did possess a coastal navy with many small gunboats and corvettes, and even a few larger frigate sized ships. Wherever they posed a threat, they were attacked, and in broad terms, the Iraqi Navy was virtually destroyed by the Royal Navy and coalition forces, having nineteen of their major ships sunk, and six others seriously damaged. There were also many smaller boats attacked and the final total of the Iraqi Navy's losses was about 100 vessels.

With the number of Iraqi ships lost, also came a corresponding loss of life amongst its sailors and those sent to man Kuwait's captured oil wells, and these were the bodies the band were often seeing floating on the waters of the Gulf. As a matter of respect to fellow sailors, *Argus* slowed to enable her ship's boats to go out and collect the bodies to bring them aboard. It was another of those jobs we have already read about that was carried out in other theatres of war and once again came to some of the band. There were also occasions when there were so many disfigured and burnt dead bodies that they were brought to the ship in underslung nets hanging beneath helicopters, the grisly cargo of bodies needing careful and respectful tending to.

Preparing bodies for burial is a far more unsavoury task than simple words can convey, especially after a body has been in the water for some time. The smell pervades all and stays locked in your memory, but it is a job that needs doing. Another important part of preparing the deceased is securing and recording dental records and any possessions they may have upon their person, so that where possible, identification can be made at a later date. It seems a simple thing, but one that will be very important to a relative in order that they can know the circumstances and final resting place of their loved one, and that they were sent on their journey with care and respect. Several times in this book, you will read about ordinary band members who have found themselves taking on this sad but much needed duty. It is another example of things you are not told when, as a young person, you arrive bright-eyed and bushy tailed at a recruiting office looking to join up and play music. It is a duty that will pass, but a memory that will stay with you forever.

After visual identification where possible and the recording of dental records where not, the bodies were put into NBC body bags, which by their nature have good seals to keep contaminants and bodily fluids inside, before being placed in the refrigeration units below decks. When circumstances allowed, a formal burial at sea was arranged by the ship's padre. In time-honoured fashion, after a short service of dedication, one of the bulgers played the 'Last Post', and from under an Iraqi flag a board was lifted and the unfortunate sailor committed to the deep for their last voyage. Unfortunately, some of the bodies were buoyant in the salty Persian Gulf and so steps were taken to ensure they would submerge and stay in their final resting place.

With the war almost over, Saddam Hussein had withdrawn his forces from Kuwait, but during his withdrawal, he had rather unsportingly ordered that the Kuwait oil fields be set alight. The huge oil fires that raged over the land spilled out smoke into the Persian Gulf, creating a thick smog that enveloped some of the ships. It created an unsettling atmosphere as it created a dark and quiet blanket around the ship, making it feel as if they were standing still in the water.

With the war eventually won, relief was palpable on *Argus*, as it was on every other ship and establishment in the Gulf as hostilities abruptly ended. One of the musicians describes almost a sense of loss at this sudden transition from danger and tension to peace and relaxation. Suddenly not having to wear your anti-flash or consider having to 'BRACE FOR IMPACT' is a difficult transition to do, or at least to do quickly. Decompression is the word, but it is far easier to spell than initiate.

Having cleaned up the ship and stowed the equipment, everyone had time to reflect on their war aboard *Argus*. Writing post-war reports and war diaries, senior officers began commentating on the band's excellent performance, and signals and letters were written accordingly to those that needed to read them. The most immediate response was from 'an admiral' back in the UK, who now the war was over wanted to know 'when he could have his band back'. Apparently, in the game of naval trumps, admirals are way up there, and so the ship headed into Dubai, where the band could be put ashore and sent back to the UK and their admiral!

Docked in Dubai, it was by all accounts a strange feeling to be wearing civilian clothes again and no longer togged up in anti-flash gear from top to bottom. There was not much time for lengthy goodbyes as, once *Argus* had taken on some stores, she immediately sailed on a humanitarian mission to help the Kurds, an ethnic group who had also been a specific target of Saddam Hussein. Some of the band watched wistfully as *Argus* sailed away through the burning oil's smoke, which still hung over the sea. Some felt the emotion more than others, as having struck up friendships and relationships with some of the crew and nurses aboard, they were no doubt wondering if they could be rekindled when back in the UK.

Once back home, or at least at their base in RAF Northolt, the band began the process of decompressing and coming to terms with 'their war'. It seems we all have at least one, and we all have equally different ways of dealing with them and our own coping mechanisms. Sadly, not everyone's coping mechanisms are helpful and positive, which can lead to negative behaviour patterns and put pressure on relationships. Discussed amongst the band was the difficulty in adjusting back to normal life, and as a result, some previous healthy relationships floundered and were lost. On a more positive note, the band and crew of *Argus* did have a thirtieth anniversary celebration in Plymouth in 2021, when it was evident that many of the ship's wartime relationships had survived – some even having progressed as a far as marriage.

At some point during their seven-month deployment, the UK's allied commander, General Peter de la Billière, came aboard *Argus* and for reasons best known to the general, or more likely his aide, visited the band accommodation. So disgusted at the poor standard that the lower band ranks were living in, he wrote about it in his own book, *Storm Command*. Frankly, if a general in charge of a war thinks it is one of those 'must include stories' from Operation Granby, then we must accept it as a Gen dit (pun very much intended).

The Gulf War made a huge impact on every member of the band who went, including Pete Best. In answering my call for information, his lengthy and wistful reply brings us right up to date with his current life in the Portsmouth area. When he is within earshot of the naval dockyard he can sometimes hear the two-tone sound of aircraft carrier lifts being tested; that haunting sound takes him right back to *his war* in the Gulf, all those years ago, and some deep-seated memories.

In wrapping up this chapter, it would be too easy to once again fall into 'the band are wonderful' stock phrases that are liberally sprinkled throughout. Whilst this book does try to make the case that Royal Marines musicians, with their humour, musical intellect and cap badge pride, are some sort of special breed, this heartfelt endorsement from the HMS *Argus* padre probably makes the point far more eloquently than I ever could. The ship's 'Bish', The Reverend Pickering, wrote:

> I know I am quite biased, but it is just an example of their fortitude, professionalism and dedication, all exemplified with their usual courtesy and good humour. A joy to work amongst and with. Thank you. Every blessing.

upper superstructure in the event of nuclear fallout. Originally, RFA *Argus* had been a civilian ship, commandeered from the Merchant Navy for use during the Falklands War under the ships taken up from trade scheme (STUFT), but then she was bought and taken into the Royal Fleet Auxiliary complement.

Once the real-world events dictated that the ship, crew and band would be heading to war, the exercise was scrapped and the Operation Telic title initiated. This brought a change of pace and training to the band ranks aboard *Argus*, including much more detailed medical skills, damage control and further firefighting. Although good firefighting regimes on a ship are obviously important as, in the event of a fire, you have to save the ship yourself, it was not lost on the band that many of them had just come from fighting fires on Operation Fresco, the recent UK firefighters' strike. The war footing also needed some personnel changes to the band complement. This was partly due to accommodation space required when the naval helicopters of 820 Squadron, with their pilots and maintenance crews, were embarked, but also to allow the musicians to function as a band in various combinations as and when required.

At about this time, Captain Nick Grace (soon to be Major and eventually, Lieutenant Colonel, Principal Director of Music RM) made considered operational decisions to make the band complement a total of twenty-four musicians, with an added drum major for marching engagements and admin tasks, and himself as the Director of Music. The combination of musicians would allow some music functionality, with the doubling up of talents and the musical abilities of the individuals filling in any gaps. Once the helicopter squadron had flown off and further accommodation became available, an additional sixteen music ranks were flown out to join HMS *Argus,* giving the band further available combinations to perform with and overall greater musical flexibility. It also help reduced the workload amongst the medical teams around the ship; it is always a welcome relief to see extra hands added to your duty roster.

One of those flown aboard later in the deployment was musician Gareth Bott, who had spent the previous few months covering the firefighters' strike under Operation Fresco. Once he had joined the ship, completed his joining routine and been brought up to date with the ship's training, he was allocated a role in the medical facility. This meant supporting the ward staff in caring for the wounded brought on board during the ground war, which included patients of all the nationalities involved. The work was both physically and mentally demanding, and not made easier with having to quickly change roles from bass player in a band to firefighter, to medic on a warship and then back to bass playing, all within a few short months. One of his most vivid memories was receiving casualties on the flight deck during a strong electrical storm. Not only were the conditions difficult, but the sheer number of casualties flown out to the ship at one time presented its own problems, with patients having to be assessed and triaged on deck before being sent down to the hospital facility within the ship.

Although it is not to everyone's liking, something about working in the medical profession struck a chord with Gareth and after Operation Telic in 2004, he transferred out of the RMBS and into the Queen Alexandra's Royal Navy Nursing Service (QARNNS). Starting at the bottom as a navy nurse, Gareth has worked his way up the ranks, got himself commissioned and is now a lieutenant commander in the Royal Navy, in charge of nurse education. In his role within the RN nursing services, he frequently meets people who were RN medics and doctors aboard RFA *Argus* during Operation Telic, and they still speak highly of the work done by the RM band members on the ship during that difficult time. Gareth's lasting memory and final comment was about the daily PT sessions he had to attend: 'It was the fittest I have ever been!'

One of the 'benefits' of being a musician in the Royal Marines is the constant encouragement to retain fitness levels that a civilian musician might not think necessary or even want. To take any doubt out of the equation, Band Colour Sergeant David Sharp was tasked with leading the band in daily fitness sessions, something he undertook with great vigour and enthusiasm. David and his twin brother Martin, also a member of the RMBS, were both well known in the corps for their liking of sport and the game of golf. Having retired to Spain, they now spend their time beating each other at golf and tennis, and playing music in the sun.

With the band now achieving the levels of fitness and experience required to manhandle stretchers around a hot deck while wearing full NBCD gear and respirators, and hitting all their training goals and targets, time could at last be found for music. Captain Nick Grace, now happy with his new band, not unsurprisingly called 'The band of HM Royal Marines, RFA *Argus*', felt he was able to signal the commodore on HMS *Ark Royal* that they were musically ready and able to fully function. This was, of course, to fully function as a band alongside their military duties and not instead of. Time for rehearsals and playing for other ships could be found, but on completion, it was back to the ward, flight deck or decontamination cabin to continue with their war role.

Another musician of that time who responded to my request for information was James Parkinson, who must have been very young at the time of Operation Telic as he is still serving, and is currently a WO1 bandmaster at the Royal Marines School of Music. His first role on RFA *Argus* during Telic was as a stretcher-bearer on the flight deck, but circumstances and manpower soon meant that he would be working in the main part of the hospital, which included the operating theatre and high dependency unit, and helping out on the wards as required.

Two of the highlights, or perhaps more accurately described as lowlights, occurred courtesy of our American partners. A nearby US Navy ship fired an errant Exocet type missile, which having gone rogue, splashed into the sea only a few hundred metres ahead of HMS *Argus*, causing some concern and much flashing of terse signals between ships. Some American pilots also failed to correctly identify 'friend from foe' ashore, resulting in British casualties, some of whom were flown onto *Argus* for care and treatment.

One of the many stories about the band's work starts with a long list of unfortunates. The first in this story was a wounded Iraqi Republican Guard soldier, who because of his injuries was on life support and a ventilator. The second unfortunate was James and his team, who had to log roll the patient at various times throughout the day. This had the effect of disturbing the gasses within the patient's body, producing the longest sounding and most eye-watering flatulence, causing James and others to both laugh and gag at the same time, something not easily achieved without inspiration of some sort. Trying to best describe the sound and smell to off-duty personnel but being met with incredulity, James made sure the doubters were at the bottom end of the bed for the next patient roll, and voila, their ears and nasal passages were now similarly assaulted and their doubts assuaged. The last two unfortunates in this sorry saga are me, for trying to find a way to adequately describe the scene, and you, for having to read it!

As mentioned by several of my interviewees, RFA *Argus* was not ideally suited to military service. Having been designed and operated as a roll-on roll-off ferry, the ship only ended up in the Royal Fleet Auxiliary due to the logistical demands of the Falklands War. Having been commandeered by the Ministry of Defence for the war in 1982, she was retained and then joined the RFA; the ship served in both the Gulf wars, both times with RMBS personnel on board. There is a well-known group of Royal Navy inspectors from the Fleet Operational Standards and Training (FOST) who visit ships to conduct tests, run exercises and evaluate if a ship is fit for service and action. Prior to hostilities in Gulf War 2, the FOST team paid a visit to the ship and having run several tests and exercises, they produced a rather scathing report. In essence, it said the ship was not suited to the task in hand (which was not really a surprise to anyone) and barely passed it fit for service. Why might this appear in a book about the RMBS? Well, whilst the FOST team bemoaned the design and conditions on *Argus*, they made room in their written report to compliment the Royal Marines band on board as 'efficient and professional', which to anyone who has come under the critical gaze of a FOST inspection team is high praise indeed!

Now with a fuller complement band under his charge, Nick Grace and the band set about spreading their musical talents and reputations around the fleet.

They undertook several flight deck concerts on other ships, including HMS *Ark Royal*. Following the usual concert format to an appreciative and entertainment-starved audience, the band showed what they could do with limited rehearsal time. Finishing the concert with a traditional Royal Navy finale of 'Rule Britannia', then the heart-stirring 'Land of Hope and Glory', the audience raised the roof and there were cheers and calls for an encore.

Incidentally, this *Ark Royal* is not to be confused with the author's first draft of the 1976-era aircraft carrier of the same name, which had huge jets, and steam catapults to throw them into the air, where they belonged. The Operation Telic *Ark Royal* was the newer through-deck carrier design, with Harrier VTOL aircraft and Sea King helicopters. At the time of writing, the Royal Navy has recently started operating the *Queen Elizabeth*-class aircraft carriers, carrying the American-designed F-35 VTOL aircraft and British Merlin helicopters. The *Queen Elizabeth* and the other UK carrier, the *Prince of Wales*, do not usually as a rule carry a permanent Royal Marines band on board, but do embark one for high-profile tours and deployments. Those ships do have their own small volunteer bands drawn from within the officers and crew, who rehearse and perform when needed for smaller occasions or for themselves for fun. Playing music can, and should be, enjoyable, so if you have not tried it then I commend it to the house.

With Captain Nick Grace and the band firmly established aboard RFA *Argus*, it is time to turn our attention to another group of Royal Marines musicians sent to Gulf War 2 under the Operation Telic banner, those with the shiniest boots on the ground.

Chapter Twenty-One

Iraq: Operation Telic Ashore

With the band working well on RFA *Argus* and seemingly covering all the bases regarding manpower, workload and musical engagements, back in the UK there was still some doubt amongst the RMBS ranks as to who else would be required to help remove Saddam Hussein from Kuwait. One of my respondents, Rich Sharp, was serving in Scotland band at the time, having just completed four months of firefighting under Operation Fresco. Having kept up his playing skills, he and some of the others were co-opted to play at the Royal Albert Hall for the Mountbatten Festival of Music, surely a sign from someone that the war could manage without them?

On completion of the high-profile London engagement Rich and his colleagues returned to Scotland band and to the daily life of a working musician. One of the band's SNCOs, Band Colour Sergeant Paul Bateman, did say that he had been nominated to take charge of a decontamination cell in the event they were deployed, but he thought it unlikely, so all the signs pointed to having that war off and maybe volunteer for the next one. Having arrived back in the band room for a morning of playing big band jazz, the band were partway through playing the Buddy Rich version of *West Side Story* (a lively and drum-filled musical extravaganza) when in through the door burst Band Colour Sergeant John Bushell.

Known as 'Johnny' Bushell around the Band Service, with his northern accent Johnny was also known for straight speaking and getting quickly to any point that needed making. Stopping the band in the place where there should have been a blistering drum solo, Colour Sergeant Johnny 'good news' Bushell announced: 'Pack your gear, you have three days before you leave for the Gulf!'

It came as a great shock and concern for everyone, not least of all for Rich Sharp as he was in the process of buying a house, which is stressful enough at the best of times with all the attendant pitfalls and setbacks that can occur, but when you are not in the country to deal with them, is even more frustrating. A short-term solution was to give his wife power of attorney so she could act for him, thereby alleviating one problem, at least.

With everyone selected to travel to the Gulf having sorted out their personal administration, Scotland band members then headed south to Stonehouse barracks in Plymouth to collect weapons. Like all quartermasters, armourers and bedding storemen, their every need was questioned before kit was grudgingly issued, but with the clock ticking down to their RAF flight, they were only issued weapons and not the desert camouflage or body armour they would need in theatre. Still reeling from their unexpected three-day notice to move, once aboard the long RAF flight to Kuwait, reality kicked in and they could actually believe it was not a joke and they, just like Royal Marines musicians before them, were now going to war.

Having arrived and been processed, they now found that they were required urgently by 3rd Commando Brigade at a place in the desert called Camp Gibraltar. The reason for the urgency was that they were to replace, or at least provide some relief for, the first decontamination team, who had been in theatre for some time already and had been working hard. The new team arrived and after some confusion, were shown to their accommodation, which was a huge Bedouin-style tent of the kind normally associated with the film *Laurence of Arabia*. Second order of service was to get kitted out in the latest war fashion of desert camouflage, of which there was apparently no shortage here in the second line of supply and logistics chain.

Something that was evidently missing from their sudden arrival in a war zone was any prior pre-deployment training for the specific role they were expected to carry out. Yes, they had their basic training and also annual refresher military courses, but now they had to learn on the job what the first decontamination team had been taught and practised prior to deployment. Another missing element was any specialised equipment and stores needed for their role, so in time-honoured creative fashion, items were begged, borrowed or, some might say, stolen, in order to get the team up to speed and equipped as soon as possible. It seems the storemen of 3rd Commando Brigade and the Medical Squadron were a lot more understanding and less clingy to their stores than those in the UK, so in due course, Decontamination Team 2 (DT2) were ready and began their in-theatre training for the role.

Having got kitted out and happy that everyone knew their role and responsibilities, the day eventually arrived when DT2 were deployed out into the Kuwait desert. There they met up with their fellow team members of Decontamination Team 1 (DT1) and notes and experience were exchanged. Having arrived at a particular grid reference, a place only 5 kilometres from the Iraq border, the teams were told to create a harbour area and consider the available options for security. Initially, they were to help secure the area until the full medical facility could arrive and become operational, so in the short term, this required them to dig shell scrapes. A shell scrape is a good description of what it is; a small hole in the ground to get the individual below ground height, with the spoil from hole piled up and compacted in front to give a slight ridge intended to give protection from incoming fire or shrapnel from exploding ordnance. This was probably something of a first for RMBS personnel outside of military training and a reminder that they were now in a live war situation.

Having secured the location until the arrival of the Commando Forces Surgical Group (CFSG), the main tented hospital facility was then set up and operational in quick time. Once established within the Medical Squadron, the unit sergeant major gave both decontamination teams a more detailed briefing and practice on how to deal with live casualties, and in particular, any captured enemy wounded that were brought in. The main thrust of the briefings was security of the hospital unit and the safety of the staff and doctors. So, if any POWs caused serious trouble and became a risk, they were to be 'taken out' without question – another sobering thought process to be gone through by the musicians as they moved quickly between the music and the military mindset. Carrying a weapon is one thing; contemplating using it on a POW in a hospital is quite another.

With the Medical Squadron fully operational, it was not before long casualties from both sides started to arrive in a steady stream. The prescribed procedure was for the casualty evacuation (Casevac) helicopter to land a little way from the tented hospital and casualties brought in from there by ambulance. The first Iraqi casualty arrived in the middle of the night and for reasons best known to the pilot, the helicopter landed very close to the tented medical unit. This caused some consternation amongst the medical staff as anyone who has been camping knows that tent pegs and lines only have a limited breaking strain, ready to give when least expected. It was assumed by those on the ground that the pilot had landed so close to save transfer time for one of our own wounded, so the decontamination teams wasted no time in rushing to the waiting chopper, ducking instinctively under the whirling blades to get to the casualty. They were surprised to find that the wounded man was an Iraqi colonel who, having been wounded with several gunshots, was screaming in great pain and shouting in Arabic at anyone who would listen and even those that would not. He was deemed wounded but also potentially dangerous, so one of the band took up guard duty with him as he was being treated. For those outside the hospital tent lying in their shell scrapes, his loud screams could be heard increasingly as the noise of the Casevac helicopter receded into the night.

Along with the daily routine of arriving casualties and security duties, one of the more frustrating elements to the war was the almost constant alarms warning of a potential Scud or NBCD attack. The Scud missile was a long-range weapon and was being used by Saddam Hussein as a last-ditch attempt to bring Israel into the war. This complication would have had serious consequences for the coalition, which included other Arab countries, none of whom could politically be seen to be on the same side as the Israelis. International diplomacy eventually won the day as Israel was persuaded to stay out of the conflict and the coalition held firm. The

Scud missiles had already claimed American service lives when unluckily, one had hit an accommodation block at Dhahran airbase, killing twenty-seven American soldiers and injuring many more, so the threat was very real. The Scud could also deliver chemical or biological agents, and since Saddam Hussein had already used that kind of warfare against fellow Arabs, that threat also had to be taken seriously in theatre. At each alarm, everyone on site had to don their NBCD gear and work in their respirators, something not pleasant to do in desert conditions but was required until the all-clear was given. The alarms were irregular but frequent, and in one day alone totalled over thirty, adding to the workload, discomfort and worry of what might happen next.

The war was in full swing when the important strategic battle for Basra took place. Both decontamination teams with Royal Marines drivers were sent out of their camp and tasked with guarding a supply point and a bridge on the way to Basra. Split into two groups and sent along the road a little way, their handover instructions were simple: 'If the enemy comes this way, shoot them, and if enemy tanks come this way, shoot them with those,' pointing to a pile of anti-tank rockets. I think given the weapons, the backblast danger zones and, as we have read, a musician needing to judge distance by the judicious use of a golf swing, it was probably the best for all concerned that Iraqi armour did not put in an appearance that night.

With a few more weeks of intense casualty and security routine under their belts, it was decided to move the medical facility into Umm Qasr, a port in southern Iraq. Under cover of darkness, the whole of the CFSG was successfully moved into the town and set up in an old customs building that had previously been occupied by the Americans. Being in a somewhat less precarious and safer position, the decontamination team members added the security of the compound to their casualty and POW guarding duties. Now much closer to the local population centre, as well as military casualties they also started receiving and treating locals, some of whom had been injured trying to escape the fighting in Basra. The most distressing of the casualties as always were the children, who needed treatment and reassuring that for now they were safe and well looked after.

With the ground war won and the defeat of Saddam Hussein, the teams and the CFSG all moved again to a place called Al-Zubayr. This would be the final rendezvous for the Medical Squadron and 3rd Commando Brigade as it gathered all its people and assets together and started to account for its lost or used stores. One of the very few benefits to a war is that quartermasters and store men everywhere get to write off stores and equipment that have already been unaccountably lost. Now, with a stroke of a pen, the books could be put right, at least for a while.

The band team members were now given another unusual task in a war zone, running a sort of mini-shop within the camp, requiring them to drive off to various places to stock it up. They easily managed this less than glorious duty and their efforts in bringing a few home comforts to those who had been living in the field were much appreciated. With their deployment in the country coming to an end, while marking time they were challenged to a football match by the green-lidded Commandos of the Medical Squadron. Rich Sharp still takes great pride in recounting how he scored the winning goal, securing victory but at the cost of offending the superfit Marines they had worked with over the last few months.

When I asked all my interviewees for a story from each of the operations to end each chapter on a lighter note, this one came out as the most unusual. Having perhaps through lack of experience dug their shell scrapes nearest to the latrines, the musicians of the decontamination teams found a steady stream of dung beetles rolling their newly found treasure from the poo trench back to their homes. The route home for the dung beetles took them through the shell scrapes, stopping off briefly to thank the trench owners for their gift that kept on giving!

In considering how to wind up this chapter, it was suggested that 'the legends of the decontamination teams be named' and I can think of no reason why not. So, legends one and all: Colin Friend, John Cotton, Karl Long, Julie Jepson (née Martin), Gareth Keachie, Tom Charnley, Dave Nevatte, Caleb Brown, Tim Seels, Paul Bateman, Eva Rose and Rich Sharp – each take a bow for a job well done!

Chapter Twenty-Two

Afghanistan: Operation Herrick

This next thorny chapter covers a very difficult, costly and controversial period of British history – the war in Afghanistan. It very much depends on your viewpoint whether it was a war, an insurgency or a fight for freedom, but assuming you are reading this book for all the right reasons, let's stick with calling it a war. It was difficult because of the distance and huge drain on resources; it was costly in terms of the lives of British service personnel who were killed or wounded; and it was controversial because of waning support from the UK public as more and more of the dead and injured were repatriated. In brief, the British military contribution to the war effort ran from 2002 until 2014, with elements from all three armed forces contributing to the personnel requirements. Given the geographical nature of the country and therefore the type of 'boots on the ground' warfare involved, the vast majority of the International Security Assistance Force (ISAF) were soldiers and marines. Our own Royal Marines Commando units took on many tours of the country, and being at the sharp end took more than their fair share of losses and injuries.

The overarching leadership was under the NATO banner, but for political reasons it was called the International Security Assistance Force. Comprising forces from many nations, including the United States, Great Britain and various European countries, the coalition approach to fighting a war was in the main less politically controversial, and militarily successful; what was less so was the eventual outcome and withdrawal, leaving many to ask if it was worth the cost. This brief potted outline of the Afghanistan War does not do justice to the complexities and political wrangling that went on to get us into the war and, more importantly, out of again it some twelve years later. So, putting the politics aside, because that is what military people must do when carrying out their duty, this chapter looks at the contribution of the Royal Marines Band Service to the war effort, a war that cost the lives of 454 British servicemen and women, with many hundreds more wounded or permanently injured.

Operation Herrick unit rotations were numbered sequentially, with the Royal Marines 3rd Commando Brigade taking the UK lead every few years. With manpower stretched to the limit for so many active combat tours, it was recognised that certain second-line roles could be fulfilled by other personnel, and so RMBS members found themselves tasked and deployed. Given the numbers of respondents and interviewees for this chapter, I have decided to encompass their deployments under the generic heading of Operation Herrick and splice in individual accounts, diaries and pictures taken more or less chronologically. This, I hope, will still give a flavour of the work undertaken by the RMBS over that whole period, with not too many feathers being ruffled or indignant letters to the editor.

Royal Marines Band Service members first deployed to Afghanistan under the banner of Operation Herrick 9, with the first cohort all being volunteers. Later deployments would require a 'pic and mix' approach by the senior Band Service management, not because of a lack of volunteers, but so that the right spaces could be filled in theatre and still leave enough musicians of the right instrument categories to service the Band Service engagements at home. Band Colour Sergeant Steve 'Rasher' Bacon was one of the first in theatre, and being one of the first, he and his fellow RMBS personnel had a slightly different experience to those who would later follow on in Operation Herrick deployments. The biggest difference was the size and development of Camp Bastion, which was the main operations base for all of the international joint forces in Afghanistan. Somewhat basic on his first tour, with most people living in shared pods and working in tents, by the time that Rasher Bacon returned some years later, Camp Bastion had grown exponentially, with air-conditioned sleeping arrangements and much better food and facilities for the troops, including fast food and coffee outlets.

The band was split into two groups, with one attached to the motor transport (MT) department and the other designated as ambulance drivers. The ambulances were essentially for the camp, to meet the incoming Casevac helicopters and to receive the casualties for urgent transport to the base hospital facility. The MT section had a completely different job, heading out into bandit country on combat logistic patrols (CLP), to deliver supplies to distant operating bases, and to provide support to the thirty-plus vehicle convoys. These convoys frequently came under attack and on one patrol when personnel were injured up ahead, Rasher and the team in his vehicle were summoned to the front of the convoy to collect the casualties and take them to a hastily arranged emergency helicopter landing spot. Within a few hundred meters of the desert landing spot, their vehicle became bogged down in the sand and so the RMBS personnel had to revert to the traditional method of carrying the wounded individual on a stretcher. The huge Chinook Casevac helicopter arrived at the location in a flurry of rotor downwash and blowing sand, and the casualty was safely delivered into the hands of the onboard medical teams. With the chopper making an operational take-off and heading swiftly towards Camp Bastion, the downwash of the rotors swept the top layer of sand away, revealing various vehicle and anti-personnel mines strewn around the site. The

Band C/Sgt 'Rasher' Bacon, Band Cpl Dave Edwards and Musician Kev Marsh in front of their vehicle.

Royal Marines Commando warrant officer who had chosen the landing site and then post-evacuation saw the mines, thought it best to not tell the band stretcher team until he saw them back at camp.

One example of bandy making the best of a bad situation and getting creative with a solution was in the issue of the vehicles they were using. The first few patrols they were sent on involved the use of a Vector armoured vehicle. The Vector vehicle, with its array of weapons and added armour, and based on the proven Pinzgauer chassis, looked every bit the part of a rugged military vehicle. However, experience soon showed it was less than effective in protecting the occupants from improvised explosive devices (IED) detonating underneath the vehicle. Having received this extra in-theatre information from those who had already experienced this issue, Colour Sergeant Bacon took the lead and looked around for an alternative and more user-friendly (safer) mode of transport. The on-site bomb disposal teams had already learned this lesson and, given their experience, were very much ahead of the curve. Having seen the results of many IED attacks and compared vehicles, they were using the much-improved Tempest armoured vehicles, with a design and underside armour that would provide a better level of protection for the vehicle occupants. It took a few days of wrangling, bargaining and gentle persuasion before the Explosive Ordnance Device department (EOD) eventually relented, and agreed that one of their precious vehicles could be lent out on a temporary basis. Once in the possession of the band teams, much of the now unneeded EOD technical equipment was removed, and the vehicle converted to the safest passenger ambulance in the camp and when out on patrol. Rules and regulations still exist even in a war zone and so for RMBS personnel to 'legally' drive this new vehicle they required an in-theatre driving test and a tick box on their records, from someone in the camp whose job it was ticking boxes. Having now acquired a vehicle better suited to the job and with team members trained to drive it, the taskings continued but with better passenger and patient comfort and safety. It is these little innovations with big potential impacts that go some way to showing how a little musical intellect combined with gentle persuasion can be added to the giant military machine to make life a little easier and a lot safer. It was a small win for Rasher and his team as they continued to develop the role they had been sent to do.

Something else that needed urgent attention was a facility for washing the blood from stretchers after casualties had been collected from the helicopters and delivered to the medical facility. It sounds a simple thing, but quite morale-sapping for front-line troops heading out into the field to have to witness bloodstained equipment and wonder who the passengers were. Another problem identified by the band team was when new batches of coffins arrived in camp, thoughtlessly stacked high on the back of an open-back truck. No one heading out on a combat patrol needed reminding how dangerous their job was, without the macabre sight of an open-back truck full of coffins parading through the camp. It was a simple problem that needed a simple solution, and the band found one; a tarpaulin was acquisitioned and the distasteful cargo suddenly became more discrete. No one is claiming that these problems and solutions were innovative or groundbreaking, just that the issues were identified by fresh eyes, and then quickly and quietly dealt with. With the coffins it was not just that a simple solution was found, but more that a potentially morale-sapping problem had been identified and quickly addressed.

Other abiding memories from respondent band members on Operation Herrick 9 are a mixed bag of interesting, sad and funny experiences, the kind perhaps not normally grouped together. The interesting involved watching the Americans reacting to an unexpected explosion and casualties just as the RMBS vehicles arrived at forward operating base (FOB) Grey. The funny included being there over Christmas and hearing that all the turkeys being sent by road for Christmas Day had been blown up and were now strewn around the site of the explosion. And a sad memory, which overshadows any of the above, was the loss of sixteen Royal

Marines during this phase of Operation Herrick. More names for RM memorials, more names to remember each year and more families' lives changed forever.

At the end of this emotional, exciting but sad deployment, Rasher Bacon and the RMBS volunteers returned home, unaware that the war would continue on for many years, and that some of them would be destined to return to Afghanistan and have to relive some of these events over again.

The main thrust of the RMBS work during Operation Herrick 14 was in the medical role as part of the Close Support Medical Regiment (CSMR). This unique regiment was made up of personnel from all three branches of the British Armed Forces, each contributing the requisite manpower, resources and expertise to keep this important medical resource operating at full strength. At its maximum time of growth it consisted of 257 personnel from forty-nine different donor units, which on paper sounds like it could be a recipe for disaster, but I am told anecdotally that this was not the case. Although constantly in a state of flux, if you take a snapshot of the unit at one point in time, the percentage breakdown of the regiment was thus: the Royal Navy 58 per cent; the British Army 19 per cent; the Royal Marines Band Service 9 per cent; the Royal Air Force 9 per cent; and other Royal Marines 5 per cent – so quite a relatively high percentage proportion of personnel when you consider the overall size of the Band Service against the other units' total strengths.

With such a diverse combination of people from different regiments, corps and backgrounds, it is easy to imagine petty rivalries or different ways of operating getting in the way, but just like my own experience in the Falklands War, the medical role tends to transcend those differences, and being patient-focused gives everyone, regardless of their cap badge, a clear mission goal. After all, the fit young Marine wants to know that if he is wounded or injured then the best possible care will be delivered as soon as possible, not delayed because 'Percy' or 'Jack' are arguing over who is the senior service. (It is the Royal Navy, by the way.)

At the time we are considering and have the most information for, the CSMR was operating under the general principals of 'providing drivers and signallers in support of the medical mission, attending casualties on the ground and providing a reassuring presence on patrols and providing healthcare in static locations'. This sounds very simple until you consider the geographical and dangerous locations in which they were operating within this vast country, which greatly increased as the fighting troops expanded their operations. In truth, it was not such a different role from those who had come before them, but was structured differently under the CSMR regime. To assist the medical mission at this time required the CSMR based at Bastion to support four main operating bases, plus an additional seventy-seven forward operating locations, with patients arriving at any of these locations by helicopter, vehicle or sometimes carried in by frantic comrades. Since someone was

Everyone was surprised that, given its lengthy absence parked on a foreign port somewhere, the unit had not been ransacked and looted for its contents. Or perhaps on inspection, the array of Western pipe and plumbing looking brass instruments seemed daunting to the Afghan customs officials, and they eventually released them for onward road delivery to the camp. With some excitement, the band members were thrilled to have the opportunity to play some music when off duty, and once they got up speed and their lips back in order, they arranged a concert in Camp Bastion. By coincidence, the 'Last Night of the Proms' styled concert coincided with a changeover period for one of the Royal Marines units based out in the field, so there was a large and appreciative audience to play for. Again, just like in The Falklands and in fact musicians deployed everywhere in the preceding decades, the morale benefits of music and having bandy about when off duty proved a real tonic to the troops.

There were several more of these successful and spirit-lifting concerts at Camp Bastion, but due to the important work undertaken by the RMBS personnel in their day role, they could not be spared to visit other forward operating bases to deliver music. Back in the UK, the Band Service hierarchy decided to send a small and compact collection of musicians under the banner of a multifaceted showband.

A small band put on a festive concert for an appreciative audience.

A smaller band needing a bigger towel!

Once again, Colour Sergeant Rasher Bacon found himself back in Afghanistan as part of this fifteen-piece dance band – very different to his previous tour. The band flew out to FOBs in a collection of Chinook and Merlin helicopters, usually staying the night, performing a concert and then flying out the next day. It reminded me of my own experience of flying to bases in Northern Ireland, but by all accounts, they were much better received than we were. Flying from Camp Bastion, Kandahar and Kabul, they covered many forward bases in their tour, entertaining and bringing a little light relief to those out in the country living under constant threat. 'A little bit of normality from home' is how Rasher describes it, allowing a brief glimpse into the emotional aspect of this music tour. One such concert at an operating base for The Rifles Regiment was postponed due to hearing a large explosion just outside the wire. The Rifles' quick reaction force went to investigate and sadly found the regiment had lost men in the explosion and the human cost of the Afghanistan War had risen once again. The concert was rightfully postponed until the next night, when a subdued audience did manage to take something positive from the music, but not without having their lost comrades uppermost in their minds.

Having experienced Afghanistan in a number of different transportation methods, Rasher's considered view is that he felt far more vulnerable flying over the country than he did when driving around it outside the wire. Whether this was due to the wartime flying antics of the pilots, as certainly operational wartime flying does release the pilots to fly their machines to the limits, or whether it was about having one's own fate in one's own hands is a matter for a late night discussion, perhaps over a glass or bottle of port.

Having arrived at the destination FOB, time to eat and sleep.

For all its problems, Camp Bastion still had room to practise your golf swing, if only to judge distance.

The musical warriors on Operation Herrick 14 continued their work and music. Other smaller combinations of musicians also flourished from within the band ranks, with a brass quintet for church services, a jazz band just for fun, and a rock band creatively called 'The Taliband'. They even played to accompany some of the civilian entertainers who were flown in to relieve the monotony of long tours, Cheryl Cole being just one of the many people you will probably never have heard of either. (Edit: I believe she is in a popular singing group from the north.)

More emotive reasons for music were also in evidence when the deceased were prepared for the all too many repatriation flights back to the UK. With respect for the fallen warriors, the band did add emotion and decorum to the sombre scene by the playing of Edward Elgar's 'Nimrod'. This is a well-known formal piece of music that has been played at nearly every military funeral that I have attended over the years, and I have been to quite a few. Its haunting melody and subtle nuances help create a suitable musical backdrop to a funeral.

I am aware that several times throughout this book I have written 'this is not about me but…' and then blatantly gone on to talk about myself. Well, this is another one of those, but one that I think is important, so will gladly take any flak for including it. For those of us at home during these many repatriations, the town of Royal Wooten Bassett became a focal point for the funeral hearses that met these aircraft and took the fallen to their final resting place. So personally touched was I at how the town gave up their time to honour our dead, I decided to write a piece of music and dedicate it to our fallen heroes and to the town of Royal Wooten Bassett. My clumsily written but heartfelt march, called 'The Heroes Return', contains a simple tune and, of course, a drum solo. Such was its impact, it was played twice, which some say was twice too often, but the thought behind it was sincere and heartfelt.

When I asked RMBS members about funny stories or dits about the tour, so many were offered up that I had to take an editorial decision on what to include, lest just like the firefighting chapter it became a light comedic festival. One of the stories I like concerns the table I previously referred to in the children's ward at Camp Bastion. One of the band members (who, to protect his identity, I shall refer to as Musician A) received a parcel addressed to him but with no note or idea as to who had sent it. The strange assortment of goods included a cigar, a baseball cap, six Fruit Shoot juices in plastic bottles and a copy of *The Cockleshell Heroes*. With the cigar smoked, the hat worn and the book read, the Fruit Shoots were added to the children's table and were at some point taken by the children and drunk. It was only on return to the UK that a fellow musician asked musician A (Richard Harvey) if he had received his parcel, read the book and smoked the cigar while also enjoying the high-quality port he had hidden in the Fruit Shoot plastic bottles!

Another standout story that I received concerns a young (at the time) bugler, Dave Birt. The reason the story stands out is that Bugler Birt was captured and held hostage, not by the enemy, but by the Australians! Having baited the hook I had better explain that the hostage taking was done in the best possible way, and for the best possible reasons.

With Anzac Day approaching, when the Australians and New Zealanders commemorate their fallen soldiers, a request came in from an Aussie forward operating base for the loan of a bugler to play at their memorial service. As a change to the daily routine, Bugler Dave Birt was quite pleased to be volunteered, and packed his kit for an overnight stay. Flying out aboard a Hercules C-130, he was met by a former Royal Marine who had transferred and was now a major in the Australian Army, and probably the reason the RMBS were asked to provide a bugler. A few hours' sleep was managed before the next leg of the journey into bandit country aboard a US Chinook helicopter to FOB Camp Holland in Uruzgan Province.

Early the next morning, the Anzac service took place against a magnificent backdrop of the sun coming up over the distant mountains, adding a certain poignancy to Dave's immaculate rendition of the 'Last Post' and 'Reveille'. Dave's playing must have impressed the Aussies, as on completion of the service and before breakfast he found himself with a tot of rum to toast the Australian fallen. He was also presented with a souvenir challenge coin and a plaque as a way of saying thank you, before packing his kit for the flight back to Camp Bastion. Perhaps it was the rum for breakfast, or the insistence of the Aussie regimental sergeant major that 'The lads want to show you their appreciation', but more likely a combination of both meant that Dave Birt missed his flight out and was now in good bad company. Another of the Aussie soldiers was also a Brit, and had a brother serving elsewhere in the country with 45 Commando. There was an issue with the Aussies getting mail across country and actually had to send it to Australia for it to be sent back to Afghanistan via the military system. Dave Birt offered to short-circuit the system and take mail back with him to Bastion, which kind offer saw him rewarded with yet more alcohol – a pattern that would be repeated throughout the day as the Aussie, American, Canadian and Dutch soldiers also dropped by to say thanks and, it appears, 'cheers'.

Having not had a drink in many months, suddenly finding himself 'lashed up' by his hosts in what was a dry country, Dave Birt was now somewhat under the weather and playing an Aussie game called 'Two's Up'. The game is banned in the Australian services, apart from on Anzac Day, when it is allowed in honour of the First World War troops who invented it and played it in the trenches in France and Gallipoli. Having now missed his flight(s) and eventually taken to his bed, Dave woke the next day feeling, quote, 'as rough as a badger's ass'. He did eventually manage to get a Chinook flight away from the clutches of his generous Australian hosts, but it was destined to fly the long way round, first visiting various mountain and forward operating bases, delivering stores and troops. The two-hour passage through the mountains, flying operationally low and fast, was something Dave's delicate head and stomach were not ready for and much to the amusement of the crew, his helmet became the receptacle of his breakfast. With the helicopter mission complete, he made it to an airport and found a C-130 flight back to his home base of Camp Bastion. As he had been gone much longer than planned, his people had started to get worried as to his whereabouts as apparently a signal advising them of Dave's Australian capture had not been received. What should have been a simple overnight trip, service and return back to Camp Bastion had turned into a four-day Australian mini-break with benefits and a badger's ass-sized hangover.

When researching this book in general and Operation Herrick in particular, one band member's name came up many times from many different sources. Band Sergeant Matt Weites was a cornerstone of the band at that time and in Operation Herrick his official role was Ambulance Response Team Leader. Due to a lack of more senior personnel, he had to operate up to the next rank level, and then because of the sudden repatriation of another Royal Marine he had to assume yet another level of supervision, 'acting up' two steps beyond his designated rank. Not only did he do this with great skill, enthusiasm and a cheerful disposition, but also his dedication and work ethic were noted as going well above what should have been required. With the above being duly noted by his senior officers, Matt Weites was written up for and received an extraordinary award, the Queen's Commendation for Valuable Service. Not only was this award well deserved, I describe it as extraordinary because it was the first extraordinary award made to a member of the Royal Marines Band Service since the Second World War. Not that the RMBS members have not distinguished themselves in the intervening years, but recommending second-line personnel for awards whilst front-line troops are out there fighting the enemy could be seen as problematic. This in itself once again gives credit to Matt Weites' award as testament to just how much he must have contributed in order to have stood out enough to be recommended, but also awarded. Matt subsequently went on to become an officer in the Band Service and is currently a captain RM, and director of music of one of the bands in the West Country.

With that broad overview of the Operation Herrick deployments, interspersed with stories from RMBS personnel who were there, I will have no doubt sold short the many other RMBS members on their work, service and experiences in Afghanistan, and if that is the case, I offer my sincere apologies. The people who responded quickest took up most of the available space and time before the editorial deadline meant a cut-off. Apologies made, I do hope that amongst the horror, danger and clumsy writing the reader will have gained some knowledge, feel and respect for the work done by Royal Marines musicians in this very active war zone.

I think the final words in this chapter belong to Richard Harvey, who, after a full career in the Royal Marines, thoughtfully and emotionally added: 'After twenty-two years in the Royal Marines, playing music and taking part in Operation Herrick, I fully realised just what my job as a military musician was all about.'

Chapter Twenty-Three

The Cyprus Reinforcement Unit

Perhaps one of the most unusual deployments for the Royal Marines Band Service occurred in 2007. It is unusual for several reasons, not least of which was the unimaginative name of the deployment. Operational names can be deliberately obscure so as to disguise any real purpose of the action, or equally creative to provide a strong name and direction, but the Cyprus Reinforcement Unit (CRU) title simply 'does what it says on the tin' and no more.

Another reason for its uniqueness was that this was the first deployment where RMBS ranks were sent as a standalone unit, and not just as additional personnel to another bigger military organisation. Usually attached to add some manpower and musical intellect to someone else's party, this was the RMBS tasked with and organising the actual party themselves.

Just how the Royal Marines Band Service found themselves with a solo military tasking echoes back to previous military operations, namely Operation Herrick and Operation Telic (now there are some proper sounding operational names!). Not only had these major military commitments stretched the armed forces, but defence budget reductions, recruiting shortfalls and the non-retention of already serving personnel had taken its toll. There were simply not enough overall numbers of personnel for the various planned military overseas deployments as well as being able to fulfil long-standing commitments such as Cyprus.

The Royal Welsh Fusiliers, who were the resident army regiment on Cyprus, found themselves being plucked from their island idyll to be sent to the equally sunny but less idyllic Afghanistan to perform fusilier type duties. One can reasonably expect that they and their families were less than thrilled. Equally less thrilled must have been the army officer who at some oak table meeting had to suggest to his boss, 'Perhaps we could ask the Royal Navy to help?' Although I am paraphrasing an already imaginary conversation, in some form or another that suggestion must have been made by someone. Once recorded in the meeting minutes, agreed and actioned, the formal request to the Royal Navy must have raised a few eyebrows, as it was cascaded down the bagatelle of the Admiralty hierarchy before finally ending up on the desk of the office called Royal Marines Band Service. For a coffee-spitting moment, the first band officer to have sight of the memo must have had to pinch himself and check he had not left the lid off the glue on his desk! No, it was a genuine warning order and the RMBS took stock of how best to service it. It was no doubt partly due to their excellent work in other theatres of operation, adaptability and military training in guarding key points that it was decided this was a task that the RMBS could undertake by themselves, perhaps even without an overarching Commando infrastructure in place. So, with that entirely speculative and caffeine-imagined preamble coming to a close, with the help of my informants and interviewees, this chapter returns to a more factual narrative.

Post-Christmas 2007, the majority of the RMBS were preparing for the annual Mountbatten Festival of Music, a prestigious event by the Royal Marines massed concert bands, held at the Royal Albert Hall in London. Once the various bands were assembled and rehearsing, rumours had started amongst the musicians of a foreign deployment of sorts with guns! To put people's minds at rest, the rumours were scotched by the band officers with a firm 'It's very unlikely we will be deploying', to be replaced all too quickly with 'It's a possibility we will be deploying', before the *coup de grâce* was dropped, 'We're going!' All doubt was cast aside following much discussion at a senior level and eventually an official 'warning order' was issued. In doing so, it set out the military requirements, which in short meant a non-musical deployment to Cyprus for key point protection of the British assets on the island.

When the details of just who would be going were released, most people were surprised to hear that the whole of the band at Britannia Royal Navy College were earmarked for a suntan, along with additional ranks from the bands at Portsmouth, Plymouth and Scotland. The surprise was added to as, for the RMBS, being in the band at BRNC was seen as a quiet little backwater, somewhere to avoid the spotlight of the bigger staff bands, the foreign trips and to be cosied up at home every night. Add to this that BRNC was the Royal Navy's officers' training facility, where all officers up to and including admirals had been trained, then for *their* band to be released and sent off with guns must say something about the available manpower and needs of that time. To fulfil this tasking, many of BRNC's regular musical engagements had to be cancelled but the prestigious annual Lord High Admiral's Parade was seen as sacrosanct, so much so that the RM band just down the A38 road in Plymouth were recalled back early from their Easter leave to provide the musical element to this very high-profile event. Given that the inspecting VIP for the Lord High Admiral's Parade was usually a member of the Royal Family, then perhaps that would not come as such a surprise.

The evaluation of the task dictated that the deployment to Cyprus would require about eighty RMBS personnel across the rank structure. It required them to all undertake pre-deployment training, which would include words seldom used in the musical world such as infantry patrolling, section battle drills, key point guarding, vehicle checkpoints and hours on the ranges passing their weapon tests on the

SA80 rifle. It was a comprehensive and lengthy training package, but with the deployment date fast approaching, it meant the postponement of Easter leave for all those involved.

Two of the positives to come out of the rumour mill at this time confirmed that they would be taking musical instruments to keep up their core skills, and that the deployment that was initially mooted to be for a two-year period was now going to be for just a few months. The relief was palpable amongst the ranks destined for Cyprus, as a two-year posting away from their beautiful Dartmouth seafront base in Devon would have been inconceivable, and for some it might have been good reason to apply for premature release from the already manpower-strapped services. But a couple of months in the sun was deemed 'doable' and with the training already underway and Easter leave banked for another day, the RMBS people just got on with it. Perhaps my writing implies that they had a choice, but the military, the Marines and the musicians of the band have little or no choice once ordered to do something; it is best just to get on with it and find something in it to smile about, even if it is through clenched teeth with rolling eyeballs.

Along with the total of eighty-three RMBS members deployed, twelve Royal Marine Commandos were attached to the band deployment, which was very different to the usual reverse routine of having the band attached to a Commando unit (which, as you have read, had happened many times before). These roughty toughty Marines were not minders or babysitters per se, but fully integrated into roles within the newly formed unit; but it was not lost on anyone that having a cadre of fully trained Royal Marines Commandos along brought a wealth of military knowledge and experience to the operation. Perhaps a bit like when a parent removes the stabilisers from a child's bicycle, but still stays close to make sure they do not fall off.

On 26 March 2007, Band Officer Captain Jon Ridley, later to be Lieutenant Colonel Jon Ridley, Principal Director of Music Royal Marines, along with the rest of the advance party landed in Cyprus and began preparations for the arrival of the main body and the handover from the army incumbents. Within a few days, the entire CRU force arrived and began acclimatising to their new surroundings and living conditions, and fleeting glimpses of spring sunshine that offered hope of a tan before the deployment was over.

Visits were made to the ranges to test and zero personal weapons, and to make sure personnel were closing the right eye when firing. Everyone was busy preparing for the big handover on what some people considered was an appropriate date – 1 April. When it came, the handover from the Welsh Fusiliers went relatively smoothly until the band replaced the Army Infantry unit flag with that of the White Ensign of the Royal Navy. The outgoing Fusilier RSM's protestations about the changing of the flags was politely noted but not actioned, and the White Ensign reigned supreme during the musicians' tenure. If you call for the navy's help, then you must expect the navy's flag! This is also a good time to reiterate that the Royal Marines, Commando and Band Service alike are all part of the Royal Navy branch of the British Armed Forces, and are therefore quite happy to use that senior service title and trump card when it suits.

The area of responsibility for the band personnel was known as the Western Sovereign Base Area (WSBA) but following a further request from the army, a little 'mission creep' crept in, and they also temporarily covered the Eastern Sovereign Base Area (ESBA) at Dhekelia. Other guarding tasks included the site at Episkopi, which along with Dhekelia would have been areas well known to members of Plymouth's Commando Forces band of the 1980s, but for much less arduous duties. When we were there, it was as a base for us to live, sleep and drip egg banjo yolks down our sunburnt bodies; none of this gun-wielding and patrolling malarkey!

As well as guarding duties, band members of the CRU also had to provide two quick reaction forces (QRF), one at five minutes' readiness and the other at thirty minutes' standby. The QRF was not just for show, as one of these did have to react and assist the local police after a dissident was arrested. It was thought his supporters would turn up at the police station calling for his release, but like most politicians, he was not as popular as he thought, and like supporters of a Sunday league football team on a wet afternoon, they were few in number.

Cyprus has an impressive mountain range and high up in Camp Troodos and Mount Olympus there were two manned satellite bases. The location and terrain provided excellent facilities for training and the Land Rover drivers (being essential should they ever need to go off road). It was one aspect of the training that the officers deemed necessary and the participants regarded as fun.

With training and settling in complete, within a few days the band personnel had assumed their responsibilities and settled into their routines and duties. Band officer Major Nick Grace was another of those officers who would in time become Lieutenant Colonel PDM in charge of the Band Service. He was the company commander, running the headquarters control room at Episkopi. He designated that the bulk of the personnel would be divided into two main troops, one of which would be the operation troop, carrying out the daily taskings, and the other a camp troop, which as the name suggests, stayed closer to home. The operations troop did the daily work, and unless there was an incident, the camp troop had the time to keep up their music skills, rehearse as a small band and catch up with their personal administration, which is Royal Marines speak for anything you have not had time to get done in pusser's time. The two troops rotated, sharing out the workload and giving everyone downtime back at base camp. It was seen that due to the nature of the deployment there was a need to keep fit, and so morning physical training and exercise was organised, along with cross-country running (the 'cross' element provided by anyone not keen on running). The same camp troop would get the weekends free for adventure training around the island, and visiting many of the ancient archaeological sites that Cyprus has to offer. From the description of the deployment it might have been seen as though there was a lot of dull guard duty, which there was, but there was also some important duty protecting the buffer zone between the Cypriot and Turkish border. There were also important British military assets on the island, with some of the key points providing important and sensitive technical support to the major military operations across the water in Afghanistan and Iraq.

The deployment was very much a mixed bag of guarding, rotation, sport, sunshine and music. Having brought their instruments and kept up their skills, within a few weeks, requests and suggestions for playing opportunities began to emerge from those who had heard of the band's arrival. First to play were the Corps of Drums, who played mess beatings for a dinner, then the string quartet provided background music for a formal function, and the jazz band played for a fundraising event. They even found the time and goodwill to play a farewell concert for the

As some are still serving, anonymous musicians of the CRU ready for patrol.

outgoing 1st Battalion Royal Welsh Fusiliers, who were going somewhere far more dangerous than Cyprus. Given the Welsh Fusiliers' name and history, the concert band featured the drummers, the big jazz band and the very Welsh Ynysybwl Male Voice Choir. Note: no matter what I do, my computer insists Ynysybwl is a spelling error!

Given their heavy deployment workload, somehow alongside their military duties, many other musical engagements were diarised, spreading the good work and music prowess of the RMBS to the uninitiated. The music portion of the tour culminated in a spectacular concert in the superb Pissouri Amphitheatre. Conducted by Major Grace and Captain Ridley, as with many RMBS concerts, it was very well received, with a standing ovation and many calls for encores from the thousand-strong audience.

I shy away from making this about me (do I really?), but it is my book and writing about a concert in a Cyprus amphitheatre reminds me of a concert by Commando Forces band during our month there in the 1980s. Marines and soldiers had to man checkpoints in the barren United Nations buffer zone separating the Turkish and Cypriot islanders. In the hot temperatures, they were rather annoyed to have to come to attention and salute any car with a flag on it, whether it was occupied by a VIP or not. During our concert in an ancient amphitheatre on the island, while the band played a piece appropriately called 'The Motor Ride', I stole the colonel's car and drove it into the arena, before getting out and saluting the flag on the front. The ordinary Marines in the audience loved the joke and gave a rousing roar of approval. The amphitheatre caretaker was not quite so pleased, though, as given there are ancient underground catacombs beneath the performing arena, the car could easily have gone through the floor! But anyways, this is not about me …

With the Cyprus Reinforcement Unit nearing the end of its deployment and with the finish line in sight, a request was made by the army to extend the RMBS CRU tour to June. This major moving of the goal posts was reduced to a slight wobble of the net by the officer commanding, setting out in no uncertain terms what that would mean both to the men on tour and to the RMBS requirements back in the UK. Good grace, adaptability and discussion eventually led to the date being reduced to 14 May, when the 'offending' White Ensign flag was eventually taken down and the operational responsibility handed back to a company of the Royal Welsh Fusiliers.

A lengthy and hard-worked deployment in hot conditions was perhaps not the most interesting for young musicians, but it seems many of them found something amidst the hard work, sport and music to enjoy, and took back with them some newly acquired military skills and experience to apply on future command courses. The RMBS ranks from Dartmouth gratefully returned to their Devon beauty spot to count their blessings and their blisters, hoping to return to their relative inconspicuous lifestyle as the Band of HM Britannia Royal Naval College.

I will leave the last words of this chapter to former Band Sergeant Richard Tilley. Richard was (and still is) a fine trumpet player and at the time of the deployment would have been regarded as 'old school'. His initial surprise at first finding himself taking part in early morning PT and then searching the scrub for illegals crossing the border was surpassed when he found himself leading patrols up to the militarily sensitive Turkish border, and afterwards in a very military manner producing patrol reports and map traces. Richard Tilley had successfully crossed that military boundary, but was looking forward to crossing back again to the musical world.

Chapter Twenty-Four

Deployment Mismusters

This strangely and arguably lazily titled chapter might sound strange to a civilian ear, but will definitely resonate with anyone who has served in the British Armed Forces. The title draws its lowly inspiration from anything in the military that was missed first time around and can then have the term ‘mismuster’ applied to it. It could be something as simple as missing the bedding storeman’s small window of mythical opening hours, thereby leaving a newly arrived unfortunate at a barracks to sleep on a bare mattress. Or, it could be as important as arriving late to a new unit or briefing, and having endured the wrath of the RSM and the ensuing extra duties, eventually catching up during a mismuster. I have been the subject of many mismusters in my Royal Marines career; perhaps the most memorable was during my initial training when, after a lengthy period of remedial swimming lessons, I was late for the actual test. There is a lot more to this unfortunate story, which you can find in my previous book. Mismusters then are a catchall for when you have missed something and someone wants to make sure you do not miss it again!

Having established just what a mismuster is, I do have to make the point that even though deployments appear under this chapter heading, they are no less important to those involved or less worthy of inclusion. They appear here either because they occurred so long ago that participants could not be found for interview, or because information on them is limited. Some of them are about incidents that were brief in time but made a deep impression on those taking part; others took up an inordinate amount of time versus the outcome. Some were so awful that circumstances demanded someone should know about them, and someone should write about them. I hope this becomes clear as we go along and that you find something in these last few stories that is interesting, sad or funny enough to be worthy of recording.

One of those unusual examples is of a role that was not a deployment as such, but directly linked to some of the major military operations written about elsewhere in the book. The role in question was not sitting locked down in a ship in anti-flash gear, or bounding across the desert in a Land Rover ambulance on a life-saving casualty evacuation mission. The important role in this case was for one of the Royal Marines Band officers running an office in support of these operations, for both the good and the bad reasons. The good was easy: moving people around to supply manpower for these operations that also took into account the personal and welfare considerations of the individual, whilst also managing 'the exigencies of the service' (which, as we have seen, covers a multitude of sins). This meant sending people to the likes of Iraq or Afghanistan for operational deployments you have read about, or to support civil organisations during the firefighter strikes, whilst also keeping a watching brief on the different musical categories left behind to fulfil the RMBS musical commitments. For example, there is no point in asking an admiral to release 10 per cent of his band for a military deployment if you then send all the trumpet players, making the band musically unusable.

The other less savoury hat to have to wear and to have to action is that of the casualty activation cell at headquarters, Royal Marines (HQRM). This is where signals would arrive from operational theatres informing HQ of those wounded, missing or killed in action. This would start an all too well-known chain of events, culminating in some poor family receiving a knock at the door with bad news. This sometimes meant that it was the Band Service officer in this role who would actually be the one on the doorstep delivering the worst kind of news. Having had a second career in the police and having had to deliver such terrible news in person, I can empathise with anyone who has to undertake such a sad task. Captain Paul Weston was one of those who for a time was in this role, and he along with Band Colour Sergeant Jan Zawada deserve a mention for their work, and more importantly, for the way in which they carried it out. In recent years, care and welfare have rightly taken on a more important role in the services, which also extends to the families of loved ones, but the dreaded knock on the door with bad news requires people with the right amount of sympathy, empathy and accurate information for them to be of use to grieving families.

One of the most unusual non-musical deployments of Royal Marines musicians occurred for one day only on 22 September 1974. On arrival at work that morning, musicians of CinC Fleet Band based at Chatham were told to get out of their issued shoes and into military boots and working rig, to assist the local police. Normally, when you hear of someone 'assisting police with their enquiries', you assume that is for nefarious reasons, but in this case genuine positive assistance was required. The reason for this sudden and unexpected change to their daily routine was that a murder had been committed at a local open recreation space called The Great Lines, and Kent Police required a large number of disciplined personnel to help search for any evidence, and in particular, the murder weapon, a knife. Under the control of the police, the musicians in line abreast painstakingly hand-searched the expanse of common ground in the hope of finding the weapon and thereby help identifying the killer. It was quite a long and tiring day, and although their work was greatly appreciated, they unfortunately found nothing of evidential value. It did however cover a lot of the area that would have tied up police resources, leaving them to undertake door-to-door investigations, so in that regard it was a success. The poor victim in this murder was a young girl called Susan Stevenson, who was stabbed and killed by a criminal called Peter Stout. Due to the excellent investigation by Kent Police, Stout was arrested, convicted and went to prison for a life sentence. It is not the first time that servicemen have been called in to assist the police with an investigation and a physical search, but it was a first for the RMBS. It must have made a lasting impression as some band members who took part still discuss it at Chatham band reunions and a few went on to have second careers in the police.

You might recall in an earlier chapter about post-war aircraft carrier deployments that you were introduced to a young, fresh-faced cello player called Richard Baker serving aboard HMS *Centaur*. On his first ship deployment, he found himself exposed to various unsavoury and exciting times, but it would not be his last ship's posting or non-musical deployment. After his commissions on HMS *Centaur*, Richard went on to have a long and successful career in the RMBS, being something of a reliable musical cornerstone in all of his postings. His musical and interpersonal skills saw him selected to play in the staff band in Deal, as well as serving as an instructor at the Royal Marines School of Music. Having made it through the ranks to band colour sergeant and settled into a comfortable band life, Richard was one of those plucked from the playing ranks and sent as a volunteer band instructor (VBI) on the Royal Navy ship HMS *Fife*.

As the VBI aboard the ship and the only Royal Marine, Richard's main duties were instructing the ship's volunteer musicians, who were drawn from the officers and sailors aboard who had previously played an instrument or were keen to learn. This disparity in the individual's musical standard is one of those things that needs careful managing as a VBI, offering encouragement to a relatively new player without diluting the overall quality of the band too much. Given every one of the band players are volunteers doing it for a hobby, and that sometimes on a small ship the choice of players is limited, it is a delicate balancing act, requiring tact and diplomacy. Richard was very proud of his own small band and considering the ship's deployment was around the Caribbean, life aboard HMS *Fife* was good, that is, until Mother Nature played her hand and a hurricane swept through the area. The island of Dominica was particularly badly hit by the hurricane and HMS *Fife* was detailed to make haste to do whatever they could to assist the local population. Richard Baker, as the only Royal Marine aboard, and a senior NCO, was put in charge of one of the motor boats to go ashore and try to repair whatever they could in terms of electricity or infrastructure. Finding a scene of absolute devastation,

Richard and his team set about their task, but it was fresh drinking water that was of immediate need, so on each visit from their ship they brought plastic containers of water to the locals. Richard recalls wondering why the plastic containers were also full on the return trip to the ship and, being in charge of the motor boat, undertook a sniff inspection. The sailors under his charge had successfully delivered the water where it was needed, but had found that the local Bacardi rum factory storage tanks were leaking, and to avoid contamination (their excuse, anyways), they were taking some of it back on board for safekeeping. Richard did not believe this (and neither will you), but in a display of leadership and matelot understanding, he helped to surreptitiously get the rum back aboard the ship and 'safely' stowed away. Having done all they could, the ship sailed and went back to normal ship's routine, but by all accounts, the next band concert went extraordinarily well, with a certain rum odour exuding from the bell end of the brass instruments.

Those who have served in any of the armed forces will have similar stories and dits to tell, especially those privileged to have sailed with 'Jolly Jack' on one of HM ships. I could fill a book (don't worry, I won't) with funny naval stories, but that would risk undermining the real purpose of this one, which is after all to record some of the unsung deployments of the Royal Marines Band Service, and remind the world just how good they are.

Some years ago, when Nelson had both eyes and before the Dead Sea even reported sick, an American admiral was the VIP visiting HMS Raleigh, the Royal Navy's training establishment. As the reviewing officer, he also inspected the band, and with his own chest resplendent in many different rows of coloured medal ribbons, he moved around the musicians asking questions about each band member and their medals. In a show of great understanding for the different way the British and Americans issue medals, on completion of the inspection he loudly told the Director of Music: 'You have a highly decorated band there, Captain; we tend to give medals away for many different reasons.' It seems that leadership and respect can cross oceans, and his acknowledgement of the band's medal count spoke volumes for this American officer. I think it is fair to say that the Royal Marines in all their forms and professionalisms are highly regarded by our American cousins but I wonder what the American admiral might have thought of the RMBS of today, dressed in their ceremonial uniforms and displaying an even finer array of hard-earned campaign medals.

Chapter Twenty-Five

An Incredible Royal Marine!

Serving and former members of the Royal Marines have a long and proud history of service to Great Britain, the Royal Navy, the corps and each other. For such a relatively small branch of the armed forces, over the years they have earned an impressive number of Victoria Crosses, an inordinate collection of gallantry medals and a corps history full of battle honours. Add to the above that the Royal Marines seem to attract people with big characters and with personalities larger than their bank balance, it is perhaps easy to see how the corps' reputation precedes it wherever it goes, hopefully for all the right reasons.

The reason for the unapologetic *Corp pissed* introduction to this chapter is that when writing a book about the RM Commandos or RM Band Service, each of us who has served knows something of the proud corps history and can also point out some of those larger-than-life personalities we have served with. We know their career path, can speak about their professional exploits and after a glass of port or two, recount their life in a shorthand of dits and 'you won't believe this but …' (insert your own RM dit here).

Of course, not everyone is a hero, a high flyer or a show-off; there are multitudes of other Royal Marines just quietly getting on with the job in the most professional way they can, and for that group it would be difficult to pick one man to represent them. Having now made it seem an impossible task, I have chosen such a man to write about, not because he was a hero in the normal gung-ho sense of the word, or because he was always funny, or on such a run ashore he 'took the admiral's daughter for a drive' (insert yet another of your own RM dits here). No: I chose this man because he crossed all the boundaries I set out in the opening chapter, from the Commandos, to the Band Service and beyond, and in doing so has an incredible career and story to be told. I like to think he represents the ordinary marine, but in an extraordinary way, so I hope you find his life, war experiences and Royal Marines career path as interesting as I did when researching it. So impressed was I that I have given this unassuming but large character his own chapter. The man in question successfully crossed the borders between the Royal Marines Cadets and the Royal Marines Commandos, and eventually ended up in a very senior role within the Royal Marines Band Service; that man was the former Royal Marines Corps Drum Major, Charles Henry Bowden, BEM.

Charlie Bowden was born in Portsmouth in 1916, into what was very much a Royal Marines family, with both his grandfathers, his father, three uncles and a brother all serving or having served in the corps. With that patriarchal heritage, and being born into the wider Royal Marines family, it was no surprise to find that at the tender age of 7, Charlie joined the RM Voluntary Cadet Corps at Eastney Barracks. Given the era he joined, the Eastney cadet unit still wore the Royal Marines Artillery cap badge, and to some degree, the unit was supported by the government and the RM barracks in which they paraded.

Having had his talents and character recognised at an early age, Charlie rose relatively quickly through the cadet ranks, spending a good deal of time as the cadet unit drum major, where he was known for throwing the drum major's mace high into the air, and mostly catching it! Before his time was done with the cadets, this portion of his young career saw him reach the unique rank of cadet unit regimental sergeant major. It seemed that even as young man, Charlie was earmarked for greater things.

An interesting but sad event occurred during his time in the RM Cadets. In the 1930s, a new Labour government decided to do away with military style cadet units, and so Charlie and fellow members had to become members of the newly styled Boys' Clubs. There were still music and uniforms of a kind, but items such as military insignia and buttons were banned. Whether this move was politically motivated or a financial decision is not recorded, but it proved to be a rather short-sighted decision, as within a few years the government would need young men with discipline and training to go and fight in the Second World War.

Corps Drum Major Charlie Bowden, BEM.

Coming to the end of his cadet career and looking at the few opportunities available to him, Charlie was keen to join the Royal Marines as a boy bugler, which he could do at the age of 14, but his father had already been down that path and for various reasons advised against it. You will recall from an early chapter that Bugler Timmins was the youngest Royal Marine to be killed in the First World War, so that may have been behind his father's reasoning, or maybe he thought young Charlie could do better playing an instrument in the band. After a lot of thought, Charlie made up his mind and forcefully stated, 'I want a rifle and a bayonet, not a musical instrument!' He would soon have his wish, as nearing the end of the 1930s, the war broke out, and young men all across the country were being called up for military duty. Once his call-up papers arrived at home, because he had come of age there was no great surprise, only the natural angst of his parents, so the only choice he had was which branch of the armed forces to opt for, which for Charlie could only mean the Royal Marines.

After some initial training at a barracks near Reading, Charlie was told he would be joining a Mobile Naval Base Defence Organisation (MNBDO), which would be responsible for protecting the Royal Navy when they were in coastal waters or bays. To defend the navy against sea and air attacks, but retaining some mobility, required a range of medium and close-in weaponry, and so Charlie was put onto the 3-inch anti-aircraft guns, commonly known as 'ack-ack'. With his three months of training completed and standing out amongst his peers, Charlie was quickly promoted to sergeant, and with his unit sent to board the liner the SS *Bergensfjord* for duty abroad. They were not told of their destination until they had been at sea for a while, which quite unexpectedly was the island of Crete. Their convoy, having dodged U-boats and air attacks, successfully reached the island and they were unloaded without incident, quickly setting up their unit's anti-aircraft and coastal defence guns to cover the bay. Not long after arriving and getting comfortable in his new surroundings, Charlie's luck and health both took a turn for the worse as he went down with dysentery – a most unpleasant infection of the intestines with a most unpleasant set of accompanying symptoms. Suffering with extreme symptoms of the disease, Charlie was excused duties and sent inland for treatment to a tented hospital facility that had been set up for Allied troops. Although getting treatment, the hospital was still very much in the war zone and was subjected to regular air attacks, which required the doctor, orderlies and patients to scramble into trenches dug along the side of each tent. Having taken cover in a trench and avoided death from above, Charlie was thinking about leaving the trench when a dark shadow blocked the sun. Covering his eyes, Charlie found himself looking up the wrong end of a submachine gun, held by a fierce-looking German soldier. 'Hands up' could be heard shouted all around the camp as patients and medical staff were rounded up by German parachutists and assembled in a central area.

Once they were all gathered, with their hands held high, one of the German officers apologised for the intrusion and gave out cigarettes, explaining that the hospital was not on the island when their air force carried out the aerial reconnaissance. Perhaps it was this conciliatory tone or that a pyjama cord needed urgent adjustment, but one of Charlie's fellow Marines lowered his hands without permission and was then needlessly shot and killed on the spot, adding another name on another Royal Marines headstone and roll of honour. Unnecessary or perhaps accidental shootings do happen in war, as I think back to the Argentine submariner who was shot by a Marine over a miscommunication while he was under guard. Whatever the reason for the shooting of the unarmed Royal Marine, it was completely unnecessary.

Shocked and appalled at the killing, and now under no illusion as to who was in charge, 300 of the walking wounded were put into a column and under the guard of six German parachutists were marched off deeper into the island. A few miles into the march, gunfire suddenly erupted from the bushes, and hearing it was a Bren gun and Lee Enfield rifle fire, to the Marines it was obviously Allied 'friendly fire'. Taking cover, the British having recognised the sound of the weapons, started calling out to the attacker. Most of the shouting was along the lines of 'STOP THAT YOU STUPID BASTARD, WE ARE BRITISH!' – probably with a few more expletives thrown in for good measure. It had the desired effect as some New Zealand Māori troops cautiously appeared from their concealed position and assured themselves the pyjama-clad 'patrol' was indeed British. Distant shouts and gunshots now confirmed that the six German guards who had run off had been found and killed. One can only hope the German who had shot the unarmed Marine earlier was one of them, and karma or justice of a sort had been served.

So now, the prisoners were free but in a difficult position. Being a mixed group with no leadership, the patients – who were from many different units and nationalities – all made their own decisions and struck out in different directions. Confident that he could find his own parent unit, Charlie set off on his own and in the darkening night followed a track heading roughly in the direction he wanted to go. After a few miles night marching in the dark, Charlie suddenly found himself challenged by a hidden sentry, calling in that time-honoured fashion: 'HALT, WHO GOES THERE?' Explaining as quickly as his shaking legs would allow, Charlie ventured close to the sentry to identify himself, and was surprised to find he was a Royal Navy sailor who was as equally surprised to find himself facing a Royal Marine wearing pyjamas, boots and a cap. His words, 'A bloody bootneck, what are you doing here?' expressed his incredulity but cemented his acceptance as friendly.

The sentry took Charlie back to his camp, where a collection of sailors were cooking bacon and eggs, which despite his delicate stomach, he gratefully accepted. Somewhat nourished and having confirmed his bearings, he thanked the 'Jolly Jacks' and set off once again for the coast, with the cheery words of a petty officer giving him little comfort: 'Watch out for the Aussies; they will shoot first and ask questions later!' Luckily, he did not have any contact with the Australians as he made his way through the countryside. After about 5 miles of walking and stumbling through the dark brush, he started to recognise his surroundings, and at first light at last found his unit's location. It was actually one of his own men that saw him first as he arrived at the dawn 'Stand to', where he was once again challenged at gunpoint until he could be identified and was able to explain what had happened at the hospital.

At the hospital, things had changed dramatically in his absence and a Royal Marines officer, Major Garrett, now addressed what remained of the unit. Militarily, things had taken a turn for the worse, and they were going to spike their anti-aircraft guns and form an infantry unit to fight a rearguard action. Now in an ad hoc unit of about 500 men, they did fight several rearguard actions against the Germans, including engaging with more parachutists, which Charlie felt bad about as they made such easy targets when slowly floating down in the valley in front of them, but I suspect his earlier dealings with the German Parachute Corps helped him and his fellow Marines overcome their distaste for the job in hand.

With the unit having done everything asked of them, Major Garrett received orders for them to surrender to the Germans on the island the following morning. Hearing the grumblings from his men and not enthralled with the idea of becoming a prisoner of war himself, Major Garrett offered them several choices, which included surrender, continue fighting in the hills or escape as best they could. Each man made his own choice, with Charlie deciding his preferred option was escaping with the major by sea from Souda Bay. Major Garrett led an escape party to the beach, which was now mostly empty as the Allied evacuation had been successful bar for a few men. Seeing an abandoned landing craft, they managed to get its engine running but with only one propeller, it turned awkwardly in circles, which was obviously why it had been abandoned. While they were busy tinkering with the engine, by good luck a fog had rolled in and covered their exposed position, saving them from the enemy strafing and bomb attacks that the men left on the beach were being subjected to. Not having the luxury of choice, 138 men crammed into the landing craft designed for a maximum capacity of ninety.

They set off, using different ways to try to keep the craft heading more or less where they wanted to go, which was towards Egypt. Having chugged clumsily throughout the night, without warning and having run out of petrol, the engine suddenly stopped, leaving them drifting in the open sea.

Charlie and several other strong swimmers jumped into the water and tried to push the huge laden craft by human power alone. One of the crew, Royal Marine Harding, adapted to the circumstances by fashioning a sail out of some old blankets, which did keep them moving, albeit slowly.

Four days into the journey, the real problem was now a lack of drinking water, made worse by the hot June Mediterranean sun beating down upon them. Once again, the ever-resourceful Marine Harding attempted a solution by rigging up some pipework and distilling seawater. This creative idea did work but only produced a few drops of drinking water, nowhere near enough to meet the needs of so many thirsty men. Getting desperate, two Māori soldiers deliberately drank seawater, which either knowingly or unwittingly caused their deaths. Having manhandled their bodies to the rear of the landing, they held a short service and committed them to the deep. Major Garrett had some stern words for the rest of the crew, which amounted to, 'If you must kill yourselves, then do it at the back of the boat to save everyone having to carry you.' Not knowing the context, it could have been an admonishment, an instruction or an attempt at dark humour to raise spirits; we shall never know.

After several more days at sea and to everyone's relief, land was spotted on the horizon and the crew earnestly began paddling and sailing to try to reach it. Major Garrett stood up and produced a can of petrol he had been sitting on for the duration of their voyage. Groans and questions about his parentage were offered up, but as he explained, the meagre 2 gallons in the can were no good in the middle of the Mediterranean, but now it would guarantee them landfall. I expect we have all at one time or another doubted an officer's reasoning or decision-making, but in hindsight, Major Garrett's early forethought appears to have been a great display of leadership.

Having at last landed ashore, through lack of food, water and exposure to the sun most of the men were unable to function, so Charlie and one other set out on a recce to try to find food, water and help for the rest of the ailing crew. They came across a pipeline, and reasoning it must be carrying either oil or water, they decided to blow it up with a hand grenade. It was a desperate measure by desperate men, but it paid off as the broken pipe did contain water and they could at last enjoy a long drink. More good luck came their way as they spotted a Royal Army Medical Corps ambulance bouncing along near them. After having told the driver of their epic voyage and escape, arrangements were made to collect the rest of the men from the landing craft. This should have been an end to their run of bad luck but as the men settled into their accommodation, which was a large tented troop holding centre, its location had been noted by the enemy. Having been spotted by the Germans and deemed suitable for attention, early one morning enemy planes strafed the camp, the surprise catching several people out in the open. One young Marine was starting his twenty-first birthday when bullets found him, and he was killed instantly. Having fought in Crete, escaped and endured the sea journey and eventually made it to Allied lines, it was a sad twist of fate for this young Royal Marine, and another name for another memorial.

After a period of rest and recuperation, Major Garrett elected to lead those that could be moved overland to rejoin their original unit, the MNBDO, which had been evacuated and was already in Egypt. Described as being 'a bit miffed' at being left behind during the evacuation of Crete, Major Garrett wanted to make a good impression when they eventually found their unit and entered the barracks, so he marched the men in and presented them to the officer in charge, Colonel Sergeant. The colonel greeted them warmly and congratulated them on their epic escape and evasion from Crete and making it back to the unit. Happy to be home of sorts, they were hardly unpacked when the unit was fallen in and told they would soon be on the move again, but this time much further east to Ceylon, to defend against the Japanese.

Having arrived in Ceylon, a young new officer was given the task of getting the unit's infantry skills up to scratch. Wanting to impress, he paraded them on the drill square with our Charlie Bowden as the colour sergeant to conduct the drills. The young officer called them all to attention and reported to the senior officer, Major Garrett. As they inspected the Marines, he presented Colour Sergeant Bowden but was surprised when the major said, 'I know what Bowden can do; I want to see what you can do. Colour Sergeant Bowden retire to the sergeant's mess for refreshments!' With that, he suddenly left the young officer to have to step up and conduct the drill session himself.

Given his experience and service abroad, Charlie Bowden was then sent home to instruct at a landing craft depot called HMS Sea Serpent. With Canadian troops a bit frustrated at having D-Day postponed by twenty-four hours because of bad weather, they were determined to leave camp and head into town – which might have compromised the security of the D-Day landings. They were stopped at the gate by the duty officer, who passed the buck and told Charlie to keep the men both in the camp and entertained. With Charlie's huge character, family history and experience of having lived through the Crete escape, he had a wealth of material to amuse the Canadians, so along with a few dits, a little rank and some military policemen, he managed to keep good order.

As the war in Europe approached its end, Charlie, being a HO (hostilities only) serviceman, did not want to return to a dull civilian job and so applied to become a full-time Royal Marine. Posted to the Royal Navy dockyard at Chatham in Kent, he had a chance meet-up with one of his old cadet shipmates who was now the bandmaster of the Chatham RN band. Remembering Charlie's cadet skills with a drum major's mace, he asked if he could stand in for him on church parade as the band's drum major was off sick. Charlie happily agreed. This simple set of circumstances led him to doing more and more work with the band until 1950, when the Royal Navy School of Music was disbanded and all the naval music came under the auspices of the Royal Marines School of Music at Deal.

Given his experience and position, Charlie was appointed as the first drum major at the staff band in Deal, a post he held for many years, and in time became the senior drum major in the Royal Marines. Liked by many and trusted by musicians and officers alike, Charlie practically wrote the handbook on how to be a modern drum major. He led the massed bands on royal parades, state funerals, Horse Guards Parade, tournaments and tattoos, as well as tours of the USA and, in fact, most of the world. He also appeared in a couple of feature films, one of which was the classic *Oliver!*, where he led a band around the square in a big musical number. Another big screen credit was the band playing the theme tune at the end of the feature film based on the popular TV puppet show *Thunderbirds* (*Thunderbirds Are Go*, 1966). The film used actual footage of the Royal Marines Band Service performing the 'Thunderbirds March' on Deal parade ground, where they stepped off to Charlie's command of 'Thunderbirds are go!'

In 1971, a new Principal of Music Royal Marines asked if he could keep Charlie for another five years, 'due to his unique experience'. Headquarters Royal Marines replied that they could not see anyone being able to do this demanding role over the age of 50, leading Charlie to point out that he was already 55 years and seven months old! Something of a compromise was reached and he was allowed to stay in post until his sixtieth birthday.

Charlie led his beloved band for the last time in 1972, playing at White City in London for a uninspiring dog racing derby on a Saturday night. He took Sunday off and then on Monday reported for duty as the beadle at The Worshipful Company of Saddlers, London.

I hope you have enjoyed reading about Charlie Henry Bowden's fascinating and dedicated career, and that I have not indulged myself too much for including it. From the Cadet band to the Royal Marines, through active war service before leading the Royal Marines Band, I think Charlie Bowden successfully crossed the military to music borders and is worthy of representing here the many ordinary Royal Marines who do extraordinary things.

Chapter Twenty-Six

Here Endeth the Book

As I come to write the end chapter of this book, I have to reflect back on whether I have achieved the aims I set out for myself and for you the reader when I started this project. I read in my early notes that I proposed to give a brief history of the Royal Marines Band Service heritage; how the line between their musical and military roles sometimes becomes blurred as they are operationally deployed; and how they have responded to and met those military challenges throughout their long history. I think I can tick off those main three aims as having been met, although that is for you to decide. So what I hope I have achieved is a series of snapshots, narrated by some of those who were there and clumsily packed into a book by a drummer's hand. What it is not and could never be is a complete history or fully comprehensive account of the RMBS's work outside of their music role.

Having had *my war*, which by now you will have realised was the Falklands War, when I was younger, I did feel rather smug that I and the Commando Forces band of that time had 'done our bit' when required, and the RMBS had at that time reached its full military potential. Of course, with that naivety of youth and lack of life experience, I was absolutely wrong in that cocoon of thought. Through my research, I have learnt that both before and after the Falklands War, the RMBS musicians gave as much as we did then, and in some cases much more, with hundreds making the ultimate sacrifice. This was brought home to me when I began researching this book, with the respondents and interviewees opening my eyes to just what their own wars and experiences were all about, and how they have affected them, which I found to be a humbling exercise. In sifting through the mountain of information readily supplied, I learnt a great deal about some of the conflicts and RMBS deployments about which I had known either nothing or only vague details. So, if only for my own edification, I am grateful to the respondents for the information, and if it has also educated and interested the reader, then better still.

I also realised that as well as the hard information I received, there were also some deep thoughts and barely buried emotions, some of which needed careful handling. I hope I have managed to incorporate some of those thoughts and memories into the book without losing the emotion. I am grateful to all of the participants for their replies, and for trusting me with their pictures, memories and, in some cases, those carefully guarded emotions as well.

The Royal Marines Band Service personnel are not front-line troops, and are not expected to fix bayonets and charge trenches, but if so tasked, I would expect them to find a creative way to do it. Fortunately for all concerned, we have professional and highly trained green beret Commandos of the highest order to do that. What the RMBS *do* is to oil the wheels of the war machine, sometimes fixing a broken part of the system with a creative solution or, at the end of the day, produce some music to entertain or raise the spirits of the fighting troops. At some time in their careers, they will each have been exposed to experiences and danger that a civilian musician could not imagine, but who one day back in the real world could be sitting next to them in an orchestra or band performing at the highest level without knowing what their neighbour's fingers have held or their eyes have seen. To misquote a well-known advertising slogan, these are not just any musicians, they are Royal Marines musicians!

To give some of idea of the high standard of some of our current RMBS alumni, I would suggest that you look at Craig Blundell – one of the world's top drummers and who tours with the likes of Steve Hackett and Genesis. Then there is the understated but huge musical talent that is Clive Dunstall, a musician and pianist who has travelled the world playing for artists such as Sting, the BBC Concert Orchestra and currently touring with a host of top-name entertainers.

Lastly, but not finally, as there are many more of them I could name, my third name-drop is Mark Upton, a trumpet player of the highest calibre, who could sit in any trumpet seat across the globe and raise an approving eyebrow from those around him. He will, of course, credit his father, Alan Upton, another former RMBS trumpet player, with first donating good genes, and secondly, good advice: to play the trumpet and not the far-too-heavy-to-carry drums!

So, whether you are a civilian who has been gifted this book by a well-meaning relative, or some hardened former RM Commando with a well-hidden but sneaking regard for your bandies, or perhaps even a young musician aspiring to join the hallowed ranks of the RMBS, I hope there has been something to interest, educate and perhaps amuse you within the pages.

I started the book by telling how King Charles II was present when the first Marines were formed. I constantly (and with some pride) reminded the reader how King George III made us 'Royal' Marines, and so to continue with the royal patronage and name-drop, I shall include this warm letter to the Royal Marines from our present monarch, King Charles III. The king, like his father before him, has graciously accepted the title of Captain General of the Royal Marines, as you will read in the gracious letter to the corps below. Having passed the Commando course himself when he was a young naval officer, he has always been a great supporter of the Royal Marines and an admirer of the Royal Marines Band Service, whether on the Royal Yacht, at Buckingham Palace, or at the Royal Albert Hall. King Charles writes:

> It is the greatest possible pleasure to assume the role of your captain general. I am exceptionally proud to follow in the footsteps of so many members of my family over the last three and a half centuries, all of whom held the role with a deep sense of admiration. The Royal Marines have a distinguished and unparalleled history, both on land and at sea. I draw immense inspiration from your courage, determination, self-discipline and a remarkable capacity to endure in the most extreme environments. I feel greatly honoured to become part of the corps family and very much look forward to meeting many of you in the near future. In the meantime, this comes with my heartfelt and special wishes for a very happy 358th birthday. *Per Mare, per Terram.* Charles.

I cannot think of a better way to finish this book than that warm message from His Majesty King Charles. So there, it's done, it's over. It would seem I have finished writing, and so you, the reader, must finish reading. As you close the cover of this book, remember that these are not just musicians; they are the Royal Marines musicians who went to war!

The massed concert bands of HM Royal Marines at the Royal Albert Hall for one of the annual Mountbatten Concerts. (*Paul Meacham*)

A Bonus Chapter

Late on in the book publication process I found myself inspired to write a poem for the Royal British Legion, to be performed at the National Memorial Arboretum during Armed Forces Weekend.

The title 'What Did You Do in the War, Daddy?' was inspired by hearing many family members saying their fathers would not talk about their war service. This led to me writing about an imaginary serviceman from any branch, war or era, first recalling how he joined up, was trained and had to fight, but then had to deal with the mental trauma of often very visceral memories. The story does conclude in a positive way, with a salute to those still serving and protecting us today.

If you choose to read it, then you should imagine the repeated 'What did you do in the war, Daddy?' question spoken in a child's voice. Alternatively, you can hear it performed with a child's voice, with added music and pictures, on my YouTube channel, a link to which is below.

The emotive music was specially written to underpin the poem and I think elevates it to another level, so credit for that to serving Royal Marines musician Colour Sergeant Andy Spain.

Whichever way you choose to absorb it, I do hope you enjoy it and find that it resonates with you.

Brian Short
https://youtu.be/6TvTmQcp24k

What Did You Do in the War, Daddy?

What did you do in the war, Daddy?

I'm glad you asked, because my early life was,
Perhaps, not quite as you think.
A bit older than you, with other young men,
I first learnt to march, curse and drink.

We were skinny and young as our names were called out,
Given press-ups and running for fun,
But it was a dark business we were preparing for,
And for that business, we were given a gun.

But *what* did you do in the war, Daddy?

I'm glad you asked, because there were good times,
With us boys now believing we were men.
We were brothers in arms and proud of ourselves,
Immortal with no thought of dark ends.

Comrades, mates – call them what you will,
I made some lifelong friends,
Some of whom only concluded those friendships
When enemy bullets brought their lives to an end.

But what *did* you do in the war, Daddy?

I'm glad you asked, because things got tough
And it's only right that you know some of the facts.
When war clouds gathered and we were called to fight,
Me and the boys were naïve and keen to act.

Like men before, we sang those songs
To grow our strength and lessen our enemy,
But it seems they had their own songs, in which *we* featured,
But as the bad guys – as their enemy.

But what did ***you*** do in the war, Daddy?

Well, I *was* glad you asked, but I regret it now
As the memories come flooding back.
We were boys to men, and quickly back again
As we faced a gut-wrenching task.

Discipline and marching both play their part
In getting a squad in step,
But when the bullets and bombs are coming your way,
You have to look deep in your heart …
And keep your head.

It's for King and Country you are taught;
That's the reason you must fight,
But when the shit hits the fan,
Then you find yourself fighting,
For your mates on the left and the right.

But what did you ***do*** in the war, Daddy?

Now I'm really not glad you asked me again
As the truth will hurt me, and perhaps also you.
Me and the boys were good at our job,
As soon our fallen enemy knew.

There was shouting and screaming as the enemy fell,
Which my training taught me not to feel,
But after the bullets, we closed with our foes,
Their end came with me thrusting cold steel.

I'm ridden with memories that should be forgot,
They are visceral and cut deep like a knife.
Somebody, somewhere, still grieves for that enemy,
Including me for taking that life.

But what did you do ***in*** the war, Daddy?

I wish you had not asked, because I really wasn't ready
To relive that previous life.
It still comes in the night when I wake in a sweat;
Never thought I'd have to say it out loud in daylight.

The demons are real and stay with me now,
It was perhaps a price that needed to be paid.
But I have the doubtful privilege of remembering it all,
Unlike my friends who gave all, and are now dead.

But what did you do in ***the*** war, Daddy?

The war? The war does not exist.
We all have our own and must meet it on demand.
The youth of a nation must decide what they will fight for,
Be it politics, their family or their land.

My own war was hard-fought in a foreign land
And left me with more memories than friends,
But that time we were needed, we all made the choice
To go forward, some to the bitter end.

But what did …

No more questions, young one.
You have asked of me and I gave you my feelings and thoughts.
What nightmares you have should be monsters and clowns,
Not caused by my time in a war.

I will say I am proud of the service I gave,
For King and Country, I did what I could,
But would I pay the price if asked to do it again? …
Yes – in a heartbeat, I would.

Now the questions are over, it's to bed and to sleep.
We rest easy tonight because good people out there
Still take the King's Shilling,
And for our peace, will a sentinel keep.

Appendix

Thanks to Respondents and Interviewees

John Ambler	Chris Archer	Steven Bacon	Kevin Baker
Richard Baker	Stuart Bartlett	Peter Best	Dave Birt
Gareth Bott	Chris Chalkley	Graham Clark	Steve Close
Nev Dednum	Paul Donovan	Paul Foley	Phil Gilbert
Phil Gordon	Nick Grace	Sam Hairsine	Rich Harvey
Phil Hawkins	Irfon Higgins	Taff Ingram	Tommy Lawton
Brian Lloyd	Paul Meacham	Mark Oliver	James Parkinson
Steve Perry	Chris Piggin	Tony Platts	Dave Prentice
John Pring	Steve Quirk	Chris Riley	Brian Roberts
Rich Sharp	Rich Tilley	William Walton	John Ware
Stu Warmington	Steve Way	Laura Way	Paul Weston
Matt Weites	Charlie Williams	Martin Williams	Dan Young

Index